To: Chuck

Vietnam: My War

Sincere gratitude!

Gene Kleese

21 May 2011

Edited by Lindsay McKissick

printed by

Jawbone Publishing Corporation
1540 Happy Valley Circle
Newnan, GA 30263
www.JawbonePublishing.com

ISBN 1590942035

A Vietnam War Time Zone from "The American Experience" from the Corporation of Public Broadcasting (www.english.illinois.edu/MAPS/vietnam/timeline.htm)

Map of Vietnam from www.sonyinsider.com/wp-content/uploads/2010/01/vietnam.gif

Table of Contents

Dedication

After I read the memories of my first tour in Vietnam. I realized that I have not given you an account of the problems I faced. I must admit these were problems of my own making and should not impact all the great people with whom I soldiered.

I particularly want to thank Jim Spears for being the best executive officer that I could ever imagine. He was an exceptional soldier and a very, very good man.

Another who helped me out when I got in trouble was Charlie Hooks, my true hero. He was our operations officer during the first tour. I had the privilege of flying with him on numerous occasions. Another, Ed Balda was the battalion X0/ S3 during my second tour and a prince among people.

My gratitude cannot be adequately expressed especially to Rodger Baker, Roger MacLeod Jack Agnew, Jim Hinton, Ed Branch, Will Pierce, Charlie Wilheight, Paul Riley, Dick Washburn, Bryan and Angie Kleese and a host of other great, brave heroes. To them and their families who sacrificed so much, this book is dedicated.

Dong Van
Yu Jiang R.
Ha Giang
Cao Bang
China
Black R.
Lao Cai
Lai Chau
Red R.
Thai Nguyen
22°
Yen Bai
Lang Son
Myanmar (Burma)
Son La
Viet Tri
Bac Giang
Hai Ninh
Dao Cai Bau
Ha Dong
Hanoi
Hong Gai
Haiphong
Mekong R.
Thai Binh
Ninh Binh
Dao Bach Long Vi (Vietnam)
Laos
Thanh Hoa
Ky Son
Tuong Duong
Dien Chau
Gulf of Tonkin
Hainan
Vinh
Ha Tinh
Vientiane
18°
Dong Hoi
South China Sea
Dao Con Co
Dong Ha
Quang Tri
Mekong R.
Chi R.
Hue
Thailand
Da Nang
Cu Lao Cham
Tam Ky
Cu Lao Re
Quang Ngai
Mun R.
Kong R.
Dac To
Kon Tum
Pleiku
Phu Cat
14°
Qui Nhon
Srepok R.
Vietnam
Cambodia
Tuy Hoa
Tonle Sab R.
Buon Me Thuot
Ninh Hoa
Ko Chang
Mekong R.
Gia Nghia
Nha Trang
Ko Mak
Ko Kut
Cam Ranh
Loc Ninh
Da Lat
Phnom Penh
Tay Ninh
Phan Rang-Thap Cham
Gulf of Thailand
Bien Hoa
Long My
Ho Chi Minh City
Phan Thiet
Xuyen Tho
Dao Phu Quoc (Vietnam)
Ha Tien
Vung Tau
Cu Lao Thu
Sa Dec
10°
Rach Gia
Tra Vinh
Hon Rai
Soc Trang
0 150 km
0 100 mi
Ca Mau
104°
Con Son
108°
©1994 MAGELLAN Geographix Santa Barbara, CA (800)929-4MAP

A Vietnam War Timeline

[Note: This timeline is an abbreviated version of the more detailed timeline posted on the Public Broadcasting System's "Vietnam Online" section of *The American Experience*.]

1945

Ho Chi Minh Creates Provisional Government: Following the surrender of Japan to Allied forces, Ho Chi Minh and his People's Congress create the National Liberation Committee of Vietnam to form a provisional government. Japan transfers all power to Ho's Vietminh.

Ho Declares Independence of Vietnam

British Forces Land in Saigon, Return Authority to French

First American Dies in Vietnam: Lt. Col. A. Peter Dewey, head of American OSS mission, was killed by Vietminh troops while driving a jeep to the airport. Reports later indicated that his death was due to a case of mistaken identity -- he had been mistaken for a Frenchman.

1946

French and Vietminh Reach Accord: France recognizes Vietnam as a "free state" within the French Union. French troops replace Chinese in the North.

Negotiations Between French and Vietminh Breakdown

Indochina War Begins: Following months of steadily deteriorating relations, the Democratic Republic of Vietnam launches its first consorted attack against the French.

1947

Vietminh Move North of Hanoi

Valluy Fails to Defeat Vietminh: French General Etienne Valluy attempts, and fails, to wipe out the Vietminh in one stroke.

1949

Elysee Agreement Signed: Bao Dai and President Vincent Auriol of France sign the Elysee Agreement. As part of the agreement the French pledge to assist in the building of a national anti-Communist army.

1950

Chinese, Soviets Offer Weapons to Vietminh

US Pledges $15M to Aid French: The United States sends $15 million dollars in military aid to the French for the war in Indochina. Included in the aid package is a military mission and military advisors.

1953

France Grants Laos Full Independence

Vietminh Forces Push into Laos

1954

Battle of Dienbienphu Begins: A force of 40,000 heavily armed Vietminh lay seige to the French garrison at Dienbienphu. Using Chinese artillery to shell the airstrip, the Vietminh make it impossible for French supplies to arrive by air. It soon becomes clear that the French have met their match.

Eisenhower Cites "Domino Theory" Regarding Southeast Asia: Responding to the defeat of the French by the Vietminh at

Dienbienphu, President Eisenhower outlines the Domino Theory: "You have a row of dominoes set up. You knock over the first one, and what will happen to the last one is the certainty that it will go over very quickly."

French Defeated at Dien Bien Phu

Geneva Convention Begins: Delegates from nine nations convene in Geneva to start negotiations that will lead to the end of hostilities in Indochina. The idea of partitioning Vietnam is first explored at this forum.

Geneva Convention Agreements Announced: Vietminh General Ta Quang Buu and French General Henri Delteil sign the Agreement on the Cessation of Hostilities in Vietnam. As part of the agreement, a provisional demarcation line is drawn at the 17th parallel which will divide Vietnam until nationwide elections are held in 1956. The United States does not accept the agreement, neither does the government of Bao Dai.

1955

Diem Rejects Conditions of Geneva Accords, Refuses to Participate in Nationwide Elections

China and Soviet Union Pledge Additional Financial Support to Hanoi

Diem Urged to Negotiate with North: Britain, France, and United States covertly urge Diem to respect Geneva accords and conduct discussions with the North.

Diem Becomes President of Republic of Vietnam: Diem defeats Bao Dai in rigged election and proclaims himself President of Republic of Vietnam.

1956

French Leave Vietnam

US Training South Vietnamese: The US Military Assistance Advisor Group (MAAG) assumes responsibility, from French, for training South Vietnamese forces.

1957

Communist Insurgency into South Vietnam: Communist insurgent activity in South Vietnam begins. Guerrillas assassinate more than 400 South Vietnamese officials. Thirty-seven armed companies are organized along the Mekong Delta.

Terrorist Bombings Rock Saigon: Thirteen Americans working for MAAG and US Information Service are wounded in terrorist bombings in Saigon.

1959

Weapons Moving Along Ho Chi Minh Trail: North Vietnam forms Group 559 to begin infiltrating cadres and weapons into South Vietnam via the Ho Chi Minh Trail. The Trail will become a strategic target for future military attacks.

US Servicemen Killed in Guerilla Attack: Major Dale R. Buis and Master Sargeant Chester M. Ovnand become the first Americans to die in the Vietnam War when guerillas strike at Bienhoa

Diem Orders Crackdown on Communists, Dissidents

1960

North Vietnam Imposes Universal Military Conscription

Kennedy Elected President: John F. Kennedy narrowly defeats Richard Nixon for the presidency.

Diem Survives Coup Attempt

Vietcong Formed: Hanoi forms National Liberation Front for South Vietnam. Diem government dubs them "Vietcong."

1961

Battle of Kienhoa Province: 400 guerillas attack village in Kienhoa Province, and are defeated by South Vietnamese troops.

Vice President Johnson Tours Saigon: During a tour of Asian countries, Vice President Lyndon Johnson visits Diem in Saigon. Johnson assures Diem that he is crucial to US objectives in Vietnam and calls him "the Churchill of Asia."

1962

US Military Employs Agent Orange: US Air Force begins using Agent Orange -- a defoliant that came in metal orange containers-to expose roads and trails used by Vietcong forces.

Diem Palace Bombed in Coup Attempt

Mansfield Voices Doubt on Vietnam Policy: Senate Majority Leader Mike Mansfield reports back to JFK from Saigon his opinion that Diem had wasted the two billion dollars America had spent there.

1963

Battle of Ap Bac: Vietcong units defeat South Vietnamese Army (ARVN) in Battle of Ap Bac

President Kennedy Assassinated in Dallas: Kennedy's death meant that the problem of how to proceed in Vietnam fell squarely into the lap of his vice president, Lyndon Johnson.

Buddhists Protest Against Diem: Tensions between Buddhists and the Diem government are further strained as Diem, a Catholic, removes Buddhists from several key government positions and replaces them with Catholics. Buddhist monks protest Diem's intolerance for other religions and the measures he takes to silence them. In a show of protest, Buddhist monks start setting themselves on fire in public places.

Diem Overthrown, Murdered: With tacit approval of the United States, operatives within the South Vietnamese military overthrow Diem. He and his brother Nhu are shot and killed in the aftermath.

1964

General Nguyen Khanh Seizes Power in Saigon: In a bloodless coup, General Nguyen Khanh seizes power in Saigon. South Vietnam junta leader, Major General Duong Van Minh, is placed under house arrest, but is allowed to remain as a figurehead chief-of-state.

Gulf of Tonkin Incident: On August 2, three North Vietnamese PT boats allegedly fire torpedoes at the USS Maddox, a destroyer located in the international waters of the Tonkin Gulf, some thirty miles off the coast of North Vietnam. The attack comes after six months of covert US and South Vietnamese naval operations. A second, even more highly disputed attack, is alleged to have taken place on August 4.

Debate on Gulf of Tonkin Resolution: The Gulf of Tonkin Resolution is approved by Congress on August 7 and authorizes President Lyndon Johnson to "take all necessary measures to repel any armed attack against forces of the United States and to prevent further aggression." The resolution passes unanimously in the House, and by a margin of 82-2 in the Senate. The Resolution allows Johnson to wage all out war against North Vietnam without ever securing a formal Declaration of War from Congress.

Vietcong Attack Bienhoa Air Base

LBJ Defeats Goldwater: Lyndon Johnson is elected in a landslide over Republican Barry Goldwater of Arizona. During the campaign, Johnson's position on Vietnam appeared to lean toward de-escalation of US involvement, and sharply contrasted the more militant views held by Goldwater.

1965

Operation "Rolling Thunder" Deployed: Sustained American bombing raids of North Vietnam, dubbed Operation Rolling Thunder, begin in February. The nearly continuous air raids would go on for three years.

Marines Arrive at Danang: The first American combat troops, the 9th Marine Expeditionary Brigade, arrive in Vietnam to defend the US airfield at Danang. Scattered Vietcong gunfire is reported, but no Marines are injured.

Heavy Fighting at Ia Drang Valley: The first conventional battle of the Vietnam war takes place as American forces clash with North Vietnamese units in the Ia Drang Valley. The US 1st Air Cavalry Division employs its newly enhanced technique of aerial reconnaissance to finally defeat the NVA, although heavy casualties are reported on both sides.

US Troop Levels Top 200,000

Vietnam "Teach-In" Broadcast to Nation's Universities: The practice of protesting US policy in Vietnam by holding "teach-ins" at colleges and universities becomes widespread. The first "teach-in" -- featuring seminars, rallies, and speeches -- takes place at the University of Michigan at Ann Arbor in March. In May, a nationally broadcast "teach-in" reaches students and faculty at over 100 campuses.

1966

B-52s Bomb North Vietnam: In an effort to disrupt movement along the Mugia Pass -- the main route used by the NVA to send personnel and supplies through Laos and into South Vietnam -- American B-52s bomb North Vietnam for the first time.

South Vietnam Government Troops Take Hue and Danang

LBJ Meets With South Vietnamese Leaders: US President Lyndon

Johnson meets with South Vietnamese Premier Nguyen Cao Ky and his military advisors in Honolulu. Johnson promises to continue to help South Vietnam fend off aggression from the North, but adds that the US will be monitoring South Vietnam's efforts to expand democracy and improve economic conditions for its citizens.

Veterans Stage Anti-War Rally: Veterans from World Wars I and II, along with veterans from the Korean war stage a protest rally in New York City. Discharge and separation papers are burned in protest of US involvement in Vietnam.

CORE Cites "Burden On Minorities and Poor" in Vietnam: The Congress of Racial Equality (CORE) issues a report claiming that the US military draft places "a heavy discriminatory burden on minority groups and the poor." The group also calls for a withdrawal of all US troops from Vietnam.

1967

Operation Cedar Falls Begins: In a major ground war effort dubbed Operation Cedar Falls, about 16,000 US and 14,000 South Vietnamese troops set out to destroy Vietcong operations and supply sites near Saigon. A massive system of tunnels is discovered in an area called the Iron Triangle, an apparent headquarters for Vietcong personnel.

Bunker Replaces Cabot Lodge as South Vietnam Ambassador

Martin Luther King Speaks Out Against War: Calling the US "the greatest purveyor of violence in the world," Martin Luther King publicly speaks out against US policy in Vietnam. King later encourages draft evasion and suggests a merger between antiwar and civil rights groups.

Dow Recruiters Driven From Wisconsin Campus: University of Wisconsin students demand that corporate recruiters for Dow Chemical -- producers of napalm -- not be allowed on campus.

McNamara Calls Bombing Ineffective: Secretary of Defense

Robert McNamara, appearing before a Senate subcommittee, testifies that US bombing raids against North Vietnam have not achieved their objectives. McNamara maintains that movement of supplies to South Vietnam has not been reduced, and neither the economy nor the morale of the North Vietnamese has been broken.

1968

January

Sihanouk Allows Pursuit of Vietcong into Cambodia

North Vietnamese Launch Tet Offensive: In a show of military might that catches the US military off guard, North Vietnamese and Vietcong forces sweep down upon several key cities and provinces in South Vietnam, including its capital, Saigon. Within days, American forces turn back the onslaught and recapture most areas. From a military point of view, Tet is a huge defeat for the Communists, but turns out to be a political and psychological victory. The US military's assessment of the war is questioned and the "end of tunnel" seems very far off.

February

Battle for Hue: The Battle for Hue wages for 26 days as US and South Vietnamese forces try to recapture the site seized by the Communists during the Tet Offensive. Previously, a religious retreat in the middle of a war zone, Hue was nearly leveled in a battle that left nearly all of its population homeless. Following the US and ARVN victory, mass graves containing the bodies of thousands of people who had been executed during the Communist occupation are discovered.

Westmoreland Requests 206,000 More Troops

My Lai Massacre: On March 16, the angry and frustrated men of Charlie Company, 11th Brigade, Americal Division entered the village of My Lai. "This is what you've been waiting for -- search and destroy -- and you've got it," said their superior officers. A short time later the killing began. When news of the atrocities surfaced, it sent shockwaves through the US political establishment, the military's chain of command, and an already divided American public.

March

LBJ Announces He Won't Run: With his popularity plummeting and dismayed by Senator Eugene McCarthy's strong showing in the New Hampshire primary, President Lyndon Johnson stuns the nation and announces that he will not be a candidate for re-election.

April

MLK Slain in Memphis:

May

Paris Peace Talks Begin: Following a lengthy period of debate and discussion, North Vietnamese and American negotiators agree on a location and start date of peace talks. Talks are slated to begin in Paris on May 10 with W. Averell Harriman representing the United States, and former Foreign Minister Xuan Thuy heading the North Vietnamese delegation.

June

Robert Kennedy Assassinated

August

Upheaval at Democratic Convention in Chicago: As the frazzled Democratic party prepares to hold its nominating convention in Chicago, city officials gear up for a deluge of demonstrations. Mayor Richard Daley orders police to crackdown on antiwar protests. As the nation watched on television, the area around the convention erupts in violence.

November

Richard Nixon Elected President: Running on a platform of "law and order," Richard Nixon barely beats out Hubert Humphrey for the presidency. Nixon takes just 43.4 percent of the popular vote, compared to 42.7 percent for Humphrey. Third-party candidate George Wallace takes the remaining percentage of votes.

1969

Nixon Begins Secret Bombing of Cambodia: In an effort to destroy Communist supply routes and base camps in Cambodia, President Nixon gives the go-ahead to "Operation Breakfast." The covert bombing of Cambodia, conducted without the knowledge of Congress or the American public, will continue for fourteen months.

Policy of "Vietnamization" Announced: Secretary of Defense Melvin Laird describes a policy of "Vietnamization" when discussing a diminishing role for the US military in Vietnam. The objective of the policy is to shift the burden of defeating the Communists onto the South Vietnamese Army and away from the United States.

Ho Chi Minh Dies at Age 79

News of My Lai Massacre Reaches US: Through the reporting of journalist Seymour Hersh, Americans read for the first time of the atrocities committed by Lt. William Calley and his troops in the village of My Lai. At the time the reports were made public, the Army had already charged Calley with the crime of murder.

Massive Antiwar Demonstration in DC

1970

Sihanouk Ousted in Cambodia: Prince Sihanouk's attempt to maintain Cambodia's neutrality while war waged in neighboring Vietnam forced him to strike opportunistic alliances with China, and then the United States. Such vacillating weakened his government, leading to a coup orchestrated by his defense minister, Lon Nol.

Kent State Incident: National Guardsmen open fire on a crowd of student antiwar protesters at Ohio's Kent State University, resulting in the death of four students and the wounding of eight others. President Nixon publicly deplores the actions of the Guardsmen, but cautions: "...when dissent turns to violence it invites tragedy." Several of the protesters had been hurling rocks and empty tear gas canisters at the Guardsmen.

Kissinger and Le Duc Begin Secret Talks

Number of US Troops Falls to 280K

1971

Lt. Calley Convicted of Murder

Pentagon Papers Published: A legacy of deception, concerning US policy in Vietnam, on the part of the military and the executive branch is revealed as the New York Times publishes the Pentagon Papers. The Nixon administration, eager to stop leaks of what they consider sensitive information, appeals to the Supreme Court to halt the publication. The Court decides in favor the Times and allows continued publication.

Nixon Announces Plans to Visit China: In a move that troubles the North Vietnamese, President Nixon announces his intention to visit The People's Republic of China. Nixon's gesture toward China is seen by the North Vietnamese as an effort to create discord between themselves and their Chinese allies.

Thieu Re-elected in South Vietnam

1972

Nixon Cuts Troop Levels by 70K: Responding to charges by Democratic presidential candidates that he is not moving fast enough to end US involvement in Vietnam, President Nixon orders troop strength reduced by seventy thousand.

Secret Peace Talks Revealed

B-52s Bomb Hanoi and Haiphong: In an attempt to force North Vietnam to make concessions in the ongoing peace talks, the Nixon administration orders heavy bombing of supply dumps and petroleum storage sites in and around Hanoi and Haiphong. The administration makes it clear to the North Vietnamese that no section of Vietnam is off-limits to bombing raids.

Break-In at Watergate Hotel

Kissinger Says "Peace Is At Hand": Henry Kissinger and Le Duc Tho reach agreement in principle on several key measures leading to a cease-fire in Vietnam. Kissinger's view that "peace is at hand," is dimmed somewhat by South Vietnamese President Thieu's opposition to the agreement.

Nixon Wins Reelection

1973

Cease-fire Signed in Paris: A cease-fire agreement that, in the words of Richard Nixon, "brings peace with honor in Vietnam and Southeast Asia," is signed in Paris by Henry Kissinger and Le Duc Tho. The agreement is to go into effect on January 28.

End of Draft Announced

Last American Troops Leave Vietnam

Hearings on Secret Bombings Begin: The Senate Armed Services Committee opens hearing on the US bombing of Cambodia. Allegations are made that the Nixon administration allowed bombing raids to be carried out during what was supposed to be a time when Cambodia's neutrality was officially recognized. As a result of the hearings, Congress orders that all bombing in Cambodia cease effective at midnight, August 14.

Kissinger and Le Duc Tho Win Peace Prize: The Nobel Peace Prize is awarded to Henry Kissinger of the United States and Le

Duc Tho of North Vietnam. Kissinger accepts the award, while Tho declines, saying that a true peace does not yet exist in Vietnam.

1974

Thieu Announces Renewal of War

Report Cites Damage to Vietnam Ecology: According to a report issued by The National Academy of Science, use of chemical herbicides during the war caused long-term damage to the ecology of Vietnam. Subsequent inquiries will focus on the connection between certain herbicides, particularly Agent Orange, and widespread reports of cancer, skin disease, and other disorders on the part of individuals exposed to them.

Communists Take Mekong Delta Territory

Nixon Resigns

Communists Plan Major Offensive: With North Vietnamese forces in the South believed to be at their highest levels ever, South Vietnamese leaders gird themselves for an expected Communist offensive of significant proportions.

1975

Communist Forces Capture Phuoc Long Province: The South Vietnamese Army loses twenty planes in a failed effort to defend Phuoc Long, a key province just north of Saigon. North Vietnamese leaders interpret the US's complete lack of response to the siege as an indication that they could move more aggressively in the South.

Hue Falls to Communists

Communists Take Aim at Saigon: The North Vietnamese initiate the Ho Chi Minh Campaign -- a concerted effort to "liberate" Saigon. Under the command of General Dung, the NVA sets out to capture Saigon by late April, in advance of the rainy season.

Ford Calls Vietnam War "Finished": Anticipating the fall of Saigon to Communist forces, US President Gerald Ford, speaking in New Orleans, announces that as far as the US is concerned, the Vietnam War is "finished."

Last Americans Evacuate as Saigon Falls to Communists: South Vietnamese President Duong Van Minh delivers an unconditional surrender to the Communists in the early hours of April 30. North Vietnamese Colonel Bui Tin accepts the surrender and assures Minh that, "...Only the Americans have been beaten. If you are patriots, consider this a moment of joy." As the few remaining Americans evacuate Saigon, the last two US servicemen to die in Vietnam are killed when their helicopter crashes.

1976-80

Pham Van Dong Heads Socialist Republic of Vietnam: As the National Assembly meets in July of 1976, the Socialist Republic of Vietnam names Pham Van Dong its prime minister. Van Dong and his fellow government leaders, all but one of whom are former North Vietnamese officials, take up residence in the nation's new capital--Hanoi.

Jimmy Carter Elected US President

Carter Issues Pardon to Draft Evaders: In a bold and controversial move, newly inaugurated President Jimmy Carter extends a full and unconditional pardon to nearly 10,000 men who evaded the Vietnam War draft.

Vietnam Granted Admission to United Nations

Relations Between Vietnam and China Deteriorate

Vietnam Invades Cambodia: Determined to overthrow the government of Pol Pot, Vietnam invades Cambodia. Phnompenh, Cambodia's capital, falls quickly as Pol Pot and his Khmer Rouge followers flee into the jungles.

"Boat People" Flee Vietnam: Swarms of Vietnamese refugees take to the sea in overcrowded and unsafe boats in search of a better life. The ranks of the "boat people" include individuals deemed enemies of the state who've been expelled from their homeland.

China Invades,Withdraws from, Vietnam

US GAO Issues Report on Agent Orange: After years of Defense Department denials, the US General Accounting Office releases a report indicating that thousands of US troops were exposed to the herbicide Agent Orange. Thousands of veterans had demanded a government investigation into the effect that dioxin, a chemical found in Agent Orange, had on the human immune system.

Ronald Reagan Elected US President

1981-85

Vietnam Memorial in Washington, DC Dedicated: Designed by Maya Ying Lin, a 22 year-old Yale architectural student, the Vietnam Veteran's Memorial opens in Washington, DC. The quiet, contemplative structure consisting of two black granite walls forming a "V", lists the names of the 58,183 Americans killed in the Vietnam War. The memorial itself stirred debate as some thought its presentation was too muted and somber, lacking the familiar elements of war-time heroics found in most war memorials.

Reagan Promises to Make MIAs "Highest National Priority": For the family members of those still listed as Missing-In-Action, the war is not over. In an address to the National League of Families of American Prisoners and Missing in Southeast Asia, President Ronald Reagan pledges to make the finding of these individuals one of the "highest national priority."

Dow Chemical Knowledge of Dioxin Revealed: Documents used as part of a lawsuit brought by 20,000 Vietnam veterans against several chemical companies reveal that Dow Chemical had full knowledge of the serious health risks posed by human exposure to dioxin, a chemical found in the herbicide Agent Orange. Evidence indicated that despite this information, Dow continued to sell herbicides to the US military for use in Vietnam.

"Unknown Soldier" of Vietnam War Laid to Rest

US Offers Asylum to Vietnamese Political Prisoners

Vietnamese Forces Defeat Khmer Rouge Rebels: An offensive launched against refugee Khmer Rouge rebels spills over the Thai border and eventually comes to involve Thai troops. The Vietnamese are successful in suppressing the rebels and solidify their hold on Cambodia despite criticism from neighboring countries and the United Nations.

1986-90

George Bush Elected US President

Vietnamese Troops Leave Cambodia: All Vietnamese troops exit Cambodia by September of 1989, paving the way for UN-sponsored elections in 1993. As a result of the elections, a coalition government is formed and work on a new constitution begins.

1991-97

Bill Clinton Elected US President

Washington Restores Diplomatic Ties with Hanoi: As Communist Vietnam inched toward market reforms and pledged full cooperation in finding all Americans listed as still missing-in-action, the United States restores diplomatic ties with its former enemy in 1995.

McNamara Calls Vietnam Policy "Wrong, Terribly Wrong": Former Defense Secretary Robert McNamara, one of the key architects of the US's war policy in Vietnam, admits grave mistakes in that policy in his 1995 memoir, *In Retrospect*. McNamara, in his book, says that "...We were wrong, terribly wrong. We owe it to future generations to explain why."

US and Vietnam Exchange Ambassadors: Ushering in a new era of cooperation between the two former enemies, the United States and Vietnam exchange ambassadors. Douglas "Pete" Peterson, a prisoner of war for 6 years during the Vietnam War, is named US envoy to the Socialist Republic of Vietnam, while H.E. Le Van Bang assumes the position of Vietnamese ambassador to the United States.

Introduction

This story is about a group of men from various birth lines and backgrounds. All were married and most already had kids. I am Gene Kleese and had joined the Army straight out of college. My wife Barbara and I drove to my first duty station at Ft. Sill, OK. There I learned artillery. After this, we went to Camp Wolters, TX for helicopter training and to Ft. Rucker, AL for cargo helicopter training. Our first division assignment was in Furth, Germany with the Fourth Armored Division.

In Jan 64, I was assigned to the 11th Air Assault Division (TEST) at Fort Benning, GA, which tested the Air Mobility concept in the hills of Georgia, and the mountains of North and South Carolinas. Those soldiers formed the core of what would become later, the 1st Cavalry Division Air Mobile. We were the 2/20th Aerial Rocket Artillery Battalion of the 1st CAV Divarty. Our Battalion was comprised of three Batteries (Company sized elements): A Battery, B Battery and C Battery. I belonged to C Battery. Each Battery was further broken down into three platoons: 1st, 2nd and 3rd Platoons. Each platoon had four choppers; there were 2 sections in each platoon. For command and control purposes call signs were assigned to each element within the Battalion. The Battalion call sign was Armed Falcon. C Battery call sign was Armed Falcon 6x. The call sign number 6 designated the Commander of each element. A Battery Commander was Armed Falcon 26, B Battery Commander was Armed Falcon 46, and our C

Battery Commander was Armed Falcon 66. Each Platoon had a distinguishing call sign: Armed Falcon 61 was 1st Platoon; Armed Falcon 62 was 2nd Platoon and Armed Falcon 63 was 3rd Platoon, C Battery.

When the word came that we would be shipping out to Vietnam in Jul 65, we headed to Mobile, Alabama on bus to board a Navy ship, the *Croatin*. We then cast off to sail halfway around the world. Only five days at sea, a boiler failed, and the ship had to limp through the Panama Canal. We then sailed north up to the nearest Naval facility, Long Beach, California.

All the men thought they would be in port for at least a week. They thought the mechanics would have to cut the old one out and do all these things... So the men all decided to go to the officer's club. I kind of instigated this whole thing. I had gone to a phone booth on the same pier we were docked on and looked up transportation. "This is Captain Kleese. I need to have a sedan take myself and my party to the officer's club."

"Yes, sir!" came the sharp reply. I realized the man thought I was a Naval captain.

"Sir, are you the one who ordered the sedan?"

"Yes, I'm Captain Kleese."

"Oh. We thought you were a Navy captain..." was his awkward reply.

"Oh well, on to the party!" I said.

The men got 2/3 smashed, partied, and then came back to the ship. Curfew was midnight. I went to bed and awoke the next morning to a thumping that sounded like the engine. I went up on deck, and found that we were already at sea. There was no chance to have another party at the Officers Club.

Except for plowing through a typhoon (a hurricane in the Western hemisphere) off the coast of the Philippine Islands, everything went fine. The days were filled with card games. You could find poker, pinochle, gin, crazy eights, hearts, spades, bridge, and even a kid's game called "pitch and bitch". I amassed a virtual fortune playing the games that abounded aboard the *Croatin*. It wasn't until the forty-firth day that I had any substantial financial loss while playing bridge. I also set a record by having seven grand slams in one sitting of bridge. Two of my grand slams were no trump!

Finally, the *Croatin* anchored (parked) about 20 miles off the coast of Vietnam, barely close enough to see their destination, Qui Nhon. On about the tenth of October, a boarding party of the advance group briefed us on our first mission which was to fly the copters to the new base, the Golf Course. We were a bit amazed at the test flight which was conducted by the 620th Maintenance Battalion personnel. The test flight consisted of picking the aircraft up to a six inch hover then setting the aircraft down and the assigned pilots boarding the aircraft, buckling in, and flying off the deck.

Ed Branch and I took off in the first helicopter, leading Paul Riley and Charlie Wilheight in the second, and Jim Spears and Will Pierce in the third. A flight of three.

As they neared the massif where the new base camp was located, I climbed through the lowest level of clouds and spied two CH47 Chinooks also racing up Hwy 19. I slammed the cyclic forward and pursued the Chinooks. About five miles from the initial encounter, the Chinooks auto rotated through the deck of clouds leaving my party and me behind. I called to the two choppers behind me to proceed on a bearing of 285° and, with a little luck and help from my navigation prowess, the three of us auto rotated and followed the Chinooks to their destination.

Below was laid out the famous Golf Course. There on the northern perimeter, the Second of the Twentieth Aerial Rocket Artillery was to reside.

The climate was tropical and monsoonal. The wet season lasted from March to September. The kratchen season was from October to March. This meant that there was always a threat of light rain and a lot of stratus clouds. (Low cloud ceilings) The rain would go away in the afternoons and come back at night, but it never bothered us when it was around.

The word came down to Roger "Bart" Bartholomew, the CO (Commanding Officer) of C Battery, that Charlie Hooks, who was C Battery's operations officer, would accompany me back to the *Croatin* to pick up some more choppers. Bart expanded the mission and sent enough pilots to fly all of Charlie Battery's helicopters to their new home. We heard about an unfortunate accident on the second night of the mission when one of the helicopters crashed into the bow of the *Croatin*. Somehow, no one was hurt, but the pilot was embarrassed and reticent to speak about the incident, as one might imagine.

The helicopters used JP4 which is the same type of kerosene that was used by everyone to light their cubicle. On the third evening, one of the crew chiefs decided to use some of the gasoline in the Huey for lamp fuel. He would have been better off had he just gone to sleep, for when he lit the lamp, he caught the helicopter on fire. He barely escaped being burned to death, but the aircraft was diminished to soot and ashes in a matter of five minutes.

First Tour

Bart

A persistent, early morning rain dripped from a slate-gray sky. Helicopters lined both sides of the An Khe airstrip, and men slowly migrated toward low fires to cook their breakfasts of C Rations. Other fires from halved oil drums serving as latrines burned nearer the perimeter. These brought a foul smelling smoke drifting across the entire strip.

"Damn! Sure wish they'd wait till after breakfast for the crap cremation," I groaned.

Bart stood about ten feet away, shaving out of his helmet, the white lather a stark contrast to a dull gray/green scene.

"They seen their duty and they done it," said Bart, wiping the lather from around his ears. "Ah, where else but in the beautiful Central Highlands of lovely Southeast Asia... And all this sponsored by the United States Army."

As the Commanding Officer of Charlie Battery, Aerial Artillery – Gunships, Bart's command consisted of regular army captains, warrant officers, and non-drafted professional solders. Discipline was not a problem. Bart knew this and treated his men with the respect they had earned.

"Gene, brew me up some coffee. And if you don't mind, smear some grape jelly on the cracker. I'm going down the line to make sure everybody's up. Thanks."

Bart smiled his crooked grin as he pulled on his fatigue shirt, barely hearing me mumble something about not being the frigging cook.

I was proud that Bart had chosen me to be his copilot. Bart was the best pilot in the unit. I had finished first in my helicopter instrument flight course (HIFC) and had set a record for both academic performance and flight performance.

Everyone was up, and most were ready. Some were conducting their pre-flight inspection, and others were already loading their 2.75" rockets. A few kidded Bart about not being a good example by sleeping in so late.

How can morale and esprit be so high in these men when things are the worst, thought Bart. Back at Benning (Fort Benning, Georgia) where they had trained, conditions were far better, but morale had only been mediocre. Now after forty-five seasick days on the Pacific Ocean and a week sleeping in pup tents, shallow bunkers and under helicopters, suddenly these men were ready to take on the world. How do you figure?

A few minutes later he briefed the aircraft commanders on the morning's air assault.

"Okay, this is a biggee," he began. "Eventually, by the second lift, an entire brigade will be involved. The landing zones, as you can see, are at the northern end of Happy Valley. As usual, we'll provide the preparatory fires and then orbit until the LZ's are secure. We'll take five of the ten ships here, Gene and I plus 2nd Platoon."

"We'll expend half load for preparatory fires and keep a half of our orbit. G2's not sure of the size of the VC force but could be as much as a battalion. An L-19 was hit by some 14.5 millimeter anti-aircraft fire over the area, so be on guard." (Actually, Bart and I were going to attack that target (VC AA Battery) during the preparation.)

"Okay, frequency for F1 (Fire net) is 35.6 fm. Also be up on Battalion Flight net on UHF and no listening to AFN on the way."

The pilots laughed and made their way back to wait in their aircraft. Like most professionals, they appeared relaxed, but their minds were already rehearsing the violent scenes ahead.

Promptly at 0755 Bart got the radio message to crank. "Fire in the hole!" I shouted as I pressed the starter button. Slowly the blades rotated, picking up speed as the engine caught. In a few seconds, optimum RPM had been reached and I picked up the chopper. I swung the tail ninety degrees right so that Bart could see that every one was ready.

They were flying UHIB (Hueys) with XM-3 rocket pods loaded with thirty-six High Explosive (HE) 2.75 inch rockets. On each door hung an M-60 machine gun, manned by the crew chief on the left and an infantryman attached to the unit on the right. These were used to provide suppressive fires as the gunships were breaking from their rocket runs. (Most people think that shooting a helicopter down would be as easy as shooting ducks, but it's much harder when the ducks are shooting back.)

As the gaggle of gunships rose above the tree line and headed east, the jungle clearing serving as the division base camp appeared on their left.

Even though only a week had passed since the division had arrived, already hovels were springing up, roads were being cut and the pattern for this small city that would eventually arise was well established. It was nicknamed the "Golf Course" in memory of better times in more pleasant places. No golf would be played here; only more serious games.

The first lift was on its way. They were scheduled to arrive at the LZ's precisely two minutes after Bart and our aerial artillery had prepared the LZ's. The crackle of commands crowded the radio frequencies, and everything was going as scheduled.

Bart made contact with the C and C (Command and Control) chopper and at 0812 began the preparatory fire.

While the 2nd Platoon prepared the LZ's, firing around the edges of the tree lined LZ's, Bart and I took aim on the suspected machine gun position.

I took over the controls of the gunship for Bart so he could resume his command duties. I began my run at 1,500 feet above ground level (AGL) and dove, pointing the gunship at the exact coordinates given to us by the S2 Intel section.

At 1,200 feet AGL I released the first pair of rockets. Slightly left of target, I adjusted accordingly. Strange orange-green baseballs were flying by me on all sides, but I didn't have time to analyze what these unfamiliar objects were as my mind was totally immersed in bringing the rockets to bear on my target.

Each pair was closer to the intended target until finally they were dead on. I switched the selector switch to four pair and again pressed the red fire button on the cyclic control.

The right rocket streaked towards the target and exploded in a fiery frenzy exactly where I had intended. The orange baseballs stopped.

"Bullseye!" I shouted, justifiably proud of my gunnery as I began my break to the left.

"Not bad, pad'nah. Not bad a'tall—especially under fire," said Bart coolly.

"What fire?" I questioned.

"Pad'nah, those orange-green things flying by were tracers from a 14.5, and I got to hand it to you, Gene you just held it steady as a rock. Cool Hand Luke."

Bart laughed.

"Damn! You mean those bastards were shooting back? Sure as hell ain't like Benning." Then, suddenly relieved, I laughed with Bart.

Meanwhile, the first lift dropped its load of infantry into the landing zone.

"Armed Falcon 66, this is Skyhawk 6 – over," announced the Red-leg Divarty Commander in the C.C chopper.

"This is Armed Falcon 66 – over."

"Roger. We've got a hot LZ here. Recommend you bounce another section or two until we get things settled down."

"Wilco."

On Battalion frequency, Bart called back to the base camp to bounce the 1st Platoon and then called the 2nd Platoon leader who was above the LZ.

"62, this is 66. Status please."

"Roger, 66. We've still got about twelve rockets each. But, at the rate we're going, we'll be dry soon."

"Okay, 62, help is on the way."

"66 and 62, this is 62 Alpha, over."

This was the call sign of the 1st section leader of 2nd Platoon. Both Bart and his 2nd platoon leader acknowledged.

"Got a small problem here. Took some fire on the second pass and my controls seem to be getting a bit stiffer."

Six two Alpha was CPT Pete Brokaw, former Syracuse right guard and his copilot was CPT Steve Stumpf, who wrestled varsity at West Point. If the controls were stiff for those two…

"62 Alpha, this is 66. Try your auxiliary hydraulics."

"Roger, we've already tried. Doesn't seem to help much."

"Okay, turn heading 180°. We'll be there in a minute."

A dirt road ran north/south in the middle of Happy Valley. A small stream roughly paralleled the road and crossed its path several times. At these crossings, the bridges had been destroyed so the road dipped five or six feet to ford the stream before rising back to the valley level.

Refugees already streamed down the road fleeing the fighting a few miles north.

"62 Alpha, 66. How are things holding up?"

There was no panic in the voice, only concern. "Not too good, 66. Seems to be getting progressively worse."

"Roger. We're going down to clear the folks off the road and I want you to make a shallow approach with a running landing. We'll pick you up and carry you home. Skyhawk 6, have you been monitoring?"

"Roger, Armed Falcon 66. We'll get a platoon over there to protect your bird until you can get a crane to lift it out."

"Thanks, 6."

Bart and I buzzed the road and sent refugees scattering. We landed nearby and by wild gesturing got the remaining refugees off the dirt roadway as 62 Alpha initiated their shallow approach.

Bart and I stood together beside their still-running ship and watched. Both of us were still attached to the radio by the communication cord of the helmets.

"Bart, I think they're going to land short in that dip."

"I'm afraid you're right, Gene," said Bart as he watched the wounded gunship only about ten feet off the ground now headed toward the arroyo-like dip.

Suddenly the gunship lurched as the pilots fought to keep it out of the hazard. Their flight now dangerously slow, the tail swung right and into a lovely palm. The entire tail section detached, drooping crazily to the ground.

Now in a wild flight, the helicopter spun. The door gunner flew out the door but, tethered by a crew chief harness, was soon lurched back inside like a human yoyo.

Bart and I stood frozen with our mouths agape. We watched as the spinning helicopter flew overhead. With its nose pointed straight earthward, it disappeared over a hill.

"Let's go, Gene!" shouted Bart jumping back into his seat.

I followed quickly. Both of us were convinced that we would be picking up remains in a helmet. We flew over the small hill behind which the crash had surely taken place. But there beside the foreshortened Huey stood two angrily cursing captains, a shaking crew chief, and an infantryman as pale as a ghost.

"Well I'll be..." said Bart as they landed beside the wreck.

"Skyhawk 6, this is Armed Falcon 66. Save your platoon, 62 Alpha didn't leave enough aircraft to save, so we're going to destroy it here. I'll take them to base and be back ASAP."

"Roger, 66. Is the crew alright?"

"Everybody's A-OK. Somebody up there must have been watchin' awful close. Out."

Now that the rain had stopped, the sky cleared. The first operation, despite its hairy moments, had been successful and a Special Forces Camp was established in Happy Valley.

CPTs Brokaw and Stumpf were awarded the Distinguished Flying Cross, though both knew that they had not a damn thing to do with landing that bird. No, someone or something else had taken the controls.

Bon Song

Endless groves of coconut trees perched on sandy plains from the low foothills of the Central Highland to the South China Sea. Here the 3rd Brigade, 1st Calvary was poised to begin its third major offensive in the two short months it had been in country. And Bart's battery was a part of the order of battle.

Bart munched on a hot dog wrapped in a piece of stale bread. The sun was out and though only 0800 hours, it was already hot.

"Boy, how do you like them dawgs?" asked Bart sarcastically.

Through a mess supply screw up, we had received 12 gross of B ration frankfurters, and the battery had been eating them for breakfast, lunch, and supper for three days straight.

"Almost as good as the ones last night, and last lunch, and et cetera, et cetera," I complained through a full mouth.

"What time is this thing going to get under way, Bart? Any idea?" I asked.

"Should be anytime. Brigade three said to expect it this morning." Bart knew it could be a little tough since NVA (North Vietnamese Army) regulars were reported as thick as fleas on a hound dog's back in the area of the LZ's.

"Is everybody ready?" asked Bart, knowing full well I would have let him know if there had been any problem.

"Yeah, they're ready to go. Ed Balda's got the 1st Platoon; Kenneth (Will) Pierce, the 2nd; and George Grady, the 3rd. Each has their assigned LZ. They're taking one section for the preparation and leaving one back for relief. All we need is—"

As if on cue, the radio crackled, "Armed Falcon 66, this is Skyhawk 3. Crank 'em up!"

"This is Armed Falcon 66. Wilco," Bart replied and then to me, "Fire in the hole!"

The seven gunships came to life. Our blades rotated at first slowly. But then, as engines caught, they spun faster and faster until the whipping of their rotors drowned out all sounds of life within 100 yards. Like great birds of prey, we rose in flight to go to war.

"Armed Falcon 66, this is Skyhawk 6. We're getting some anti-aircraft fire about two clicks (kilometers) short of LZ Beta. Recommend you proceed at tree top level until we can take it out. Over."

"Roger, 6. We'll drop down to tree top."

"Armed Falcon flight, did you monitor?"

All the platoons acknowledged.

"Holy cow! Did you see that?" I exclaimed.

We had passed over a half mile long trench filled with NVA in their green uniforms and pith helmets, all armed to the teeth. The blister crack of small arms fire sounded like a typewriter tapping an urgent warning of danger; the occasional crump of rounds finding their mark punctuated the sentence with a loud exclamation point. Seven times our sentence was punctuated.

"Skyhawk 5, this is Armed Falcon 66. Got a fire mission for conventional artillery. Over."

"Roger, 66. Switch to F-2. Red-leg Alpha will take your fire mission.

Quickly, Bart switched frequencies as I continued to fly, skimming the coconut palms.

"Red-leg three Alpha, Armed Falcon 66, Fire mission, over."

"Send your mission, 66."

Bart gave the fire mission order. Soon, behind them, field artillery shells showered over the trench.

Once again, a fresh burst of blister cracks with even more crumps. "Dammit, Bart, flying through these coconut palms is bad enough without anyone shooting at us. I vote we go to 1,500 feet and take our chance with the AA gun."

"Okay, let's go!" agreed Bart. "Armed Falcon flight let's go to 1,500 feet and get out of this fire."

The flight assembled and proceeded to the LZ's. I was relieved by Bart's decision to ascend above the "kill zone."

"Armed Falcon 66, this is Skyhawk 6. Over."

"Go ahead, Skyhawk."

"Roger, 66. We've got a Chinook down at coordinates Alpha Tango 646 325. Can you provide cover until we can get some troops in there? Over."

"Sure, I'll detach a section."

"Armed Falcon 62, this is 66. Over."

"66, we copied. Good luck with the assault."

"Thanks, 62. Let us know if you need help."

"Wilco, 66."

Over the broad plain the helicopters flew. The LZ's

were cold. Meanwhile, at the downed Chinook site, the NVA were making things hot; mortars, RPG's, and small arms fire were directed at the crippled craft. Despite the fact that the Chinook had been hauling two M120 Howitzers, the bird was so badly damaged that they could not be deployed.

"Armed Falcon 66, this is 62. Over."

"Go ahead, 62."

"Roger. We're about out of rockets. Each of us have only 4 left. Chinooks and crew are still in danger. Recommend you send up another section to help and to provide fire for the grunts coming."

"Wilco, 62. 63 is on the way. Continue to support until 63 is on station. If possible, hold your eight rounds until the infantry arrives."

"Wilco, 66."

Within 10 minutes, the lift ships carrying the infantry arrived on the scene. The impromptu air assault operation went off without a hitch. 62 and 63 provided the firepower.

Bart, Armed Falcon 66, was pleased. Only a short two months had passed since the division had arrived, but already it was proving that this new concept of air mobility was becoming a major force on the battlefield, even against a well-trained and determined enemy.

Norm

Norm Leikem was Armed Falcon 46, CO of B Battery, 2/20th Aerial Artillery. Back in Benning he was in C Battery, but that was because everyone except the Headquarters types were in the C Battery. He came from Nebraska and epitomized all the good traits of Midwesterners, especially the work ethic. He also was a loving husband to Shirley and a devoted father of a two-year-old son.

Norm had arrived at the Battalion before me and was initially part of C Battery. He and the C Battery team trained at Ft. Benning and on the wilds of South Carolina and North Carolina. During this time, when we were in the field Barbara (my wife) and Shirley (Norm's wife) set up support groups that would last long after the 1st Cavalry Division had deployed to RVN (the Republic of Vietnam).

In early July, the 1st Cavalry Division filled up with officers and men of the 3rd Infantry Division, which was also stationed at Ft. Benning. By the first week in July, we were as ready as we were going to be. Norm took command of B Battery, and I continued in C Battery. Norm was deployed in the advance party and arrived in RVN in July. Those of us who deployed by ship didn't arrive until September.

"Hey! Are you going to Mass this Sunday or are you going to sit on your butt all day?" I said as I entered his tent.

"Okay! Okay! Pipe down! You're going to wake up the entire battalion."

"Look, the only reason I go to Mass with you is for the Sunday lunch your mess sergeant puts out. Best in the division."

"Good point. Come on. We're going to be late."

I attended Mass with Norm every Sunday that we both were in camp. After church, we would eat lunch and play cribbage; most of the time our games would last into the late afternoon, when we would retire to write letters or to nap.

Everyone liked Norm. Norm was a very good Battery Commander (BC), and his troops would have gone to hell and back for him. His battery had already distinguished themselves at Pleiku and the Five Fingers battle. No doubt, along with Bart, Norm would get a battalion soon and eventually pin on stars. But it was not to be.

Late October found C Battery at the Golf Course and B Battery at Pleiku, a strategic post on Hwy 19. It was along that route that the Viet Minh had cut the French Force in two, at the end of French occupation. Norm's Battery was doing great work.

On October 21, 1965, Bart approached me as I waited at the An Khe strip for fire mission from the 1/7th Infantry who were conducting operations again in Happy Valley.

"Gene, Norm's dead."

Those three words fell like a heavy sledge smashing to the core of my heart.

"No, it can't be."

"I'm sorry," said Bart. "God knows how I loved

him. But you two… I don't know. It's so rare that two men, whom I consider to be so courageous, so brave, so good, can become such close friends."

"How did it happen, Bart?" I said, choking in my sudden grief.

"Last night, they got a fire mission about midnight. You know Norm; he grabbed his helmet and went with the section on alert. They took a ¾ ton truck to the choppers that were parked near the ammo area. A guard on the line went berserk and fired an entire clip of M16 ammo into the back of the truck. Norm was the only one hit, and he got it in the heart. The doctors said he died instantaneously."

"Oh, God," I moaned. "He was so good."

"I can arrange it to have you accompany the body home to Shirley. How about letting me know about 14:00 on how you feel about that."

"Bart thanks. You are a true friend; but, taking Norm to Shirley would be too much for me. I'll write her a letter to explain, but I think you all need me here. And, for right now, I need to be here. But… thanks."

The next day, C Battery was briefed on plans to enter the Ia Drang River Valley to intercept supplies to the VC.

Charlie Wilheight

Charlie Wilheight was a grizzled old cigar-smoking veteran who relied on his superior flying skills and his veteran status to get him through most hairy situations. But this time, Ed Balda and I had put him in a place where, even with all the skill and courage in him, he would not come through unscathed.

The place was a small pit-stop on Highway 1 about 45 miles north of Qui Nhon. It was late October. Bart flew an L 19 fixed wing aircraft over the foreboding mountains and plains of Alligator Valley. Charlie Wilheight was with Ed Balda, and Ed Branch was flying with me.

"64, this is 66. I've got a "Charlie" with some supplies and an ammo can running along a north-south south Dike. 64, can you confirm?"

"Yes 66, I confirm. Do you want us to take him out?"

"That's affirm, 64. I'll sit up here and watch the show."

Ed Branch turned to me as we eased up to 1,200 feet AGL. "Don't you think this is a helluva waste of ammunition?" he asked as we neared our altitude.

"Well, Ed, I think that the whole damn war is a waste of ammunition."

I eased the cyclic forward. There was the target, and I adjusted the trim. This last step was totally necessary, for if I'd fired while the aircraft was out of trim, there was no telling where they would land.

"Overs and shorts, and overs and shorts."

"64, right behind you." Ed Balda broadcasted.

I pulled hard right and climbed as high as I could. 61 fell to my rear and formed a mini daisy chain. Again rockets fell over and short – they were only six pound rockets with a killing radius of about 2 feet. The VC, in the meantime, had reached his destination. Both Ed and I practically hovered above the small palm and accompanying bush.

Out of the hole came the courageous VC wielding an M60 Machine Gun. (I still see that grinning VC in my sleep.) Ed Balda was close, so he got it first. Charlie Wilheight was hit in the back of his thigh. Now it was my turn. The first rounds shot out the chin bubbles. The second machine gun burst shot out some of the radios. The last rounds smashed into the engine compartment.

"How is Wilheight?" I shouted above the din. "Use all the T-shirts and try to get the bleeding stopped. Use your belt as a tourniquet. And keep him awake and take him to the Medical Center at Qui Nhon. We're hit pretty badly, so wish us luck on getting home safely."

"61, this is 66. I'll meet Wilheight there." Bart announced. "I thought you might like to know, I used some Tac Air A1E's to finish the job."

I then focused on getting my wounded bird home. A small gasoline fire had started in the engine department. I was losing power quickly. Camp came suddenly into view. I was home after an uneventful landing. I counted 75 bullet holes in our helicopter after landing.

I visited Charlie that evening. He was drugged, and his wound was still draining, but he was pretty well off. The next day, he was medevac'd to the States. I ran into him again at Ft. Rucker about a year after he'd been wounded. He was an instructor pilot at Ft. Rucker, and, all in all, he was in great shape. Except for his built-up shoe, Charlie looked good and walked without any noticeable limp. Both of us went to the Officer's Club to drink a beer to celebrate his recovery.

Ia Drang

A rather unimpressive river flows from Laos into a sparsely vegetated plain at the base of a huge volcanic massif called Chu Pong Mountain. A parallel trail had been worn bare by thousands of soldiers toting their loads of supplies to feed and equip the VC of the Central Highlands. A battalion-sized assault was planned to act as the hammer of an "anvil and hammer" maneuver to smash the VC in the area and interdict the supply line.

The plan was the farthest thing from my mind that early November 14th morning as Bart and I sat in our chopper in Plei Me - Special Forces Camp consuming a nutritious breakfast of C rations crackers and jelly. My section was in reserve. Dick Washburn and his 3rd platoon would fire the preparation fires and cover the battalion insertion into LZ X-Ray.

I considered this a break and was prepared to take advantage. Following breakfast, I turned to the radio to pick up the first lift. Dick was doing his usual professional job, and the first Company of Infantry was on the ground and reported a cold LZ (no fire received).

I breathed a sigh of relief, even more convinced that I would enjoy a peaceful, uneventful day in the beautiful Central Highlands.

Meanwhile, the infantry at LZ X-Ray conducted a cloverleaf operation to secure their perimeter and establish a picket line. That was when things unraveled.

A single NVA soldier watched with awe the lift of the US Infantry into LZ X-Ray. Then, after firing a clip of AK 47 rounds at the soldiers, he ran toward the tall Chu Pong Mountain.

The entire platoon abandoned their cloverleaf mission and entered in close pursuit. Through low brush and thick grass, they crossed through a dry streambed and onto a knoll.

He got away. More importantly, he inadvertently put the platoon into a dangerous position.

For the first time in the war's bloody history, the regular US Army troops would encounter regular Army troops of North Vietnam. A real humdinger of a fight would ensue.

The NVA force (probably a division) had been building its strength at their base camp in the Chu Pong Mountains for months. Their mission was to assist the local VC in cutting Hwy 19, which ran through Pleiku and An Khe and finally to Qui Nhon; thus, dividing South Vietnam in two—the same strategy that had been successful with the French in the early 60's.

Now with their base camp threatened, they reacted like mad hornets. Down the dry streambed they charged and cut off the US platoon. A murderous firefight began, with Dick and his platoon providing close in fire support.

Dick called Bart who was listening on the radio in our helicopter at Plei Me.

"Armed Falcon 66, this is Armed Falcon63. We need some back up. We're both about out of rockets."

"Roger, 63. 62, did you monitor?"

"I got it, 66. We're on our way."

Conventional Artillery and Close Air Support from the Air Force were also called in and directed by the Fire Direction Officer (FDO) with the 1st Battalion, 7th Cavalry Regiment. The problem was that, because of Chu Pong Mountain and the restriction governing over flight of Laotian Territory, the dive angles were too steep to allow the Air Force to maximize their firepower on the dry streambed. The conventional artillery - mostly 105 mm - was almost 10 km from the LZ. Therefore, they could only fire low angle fire, which had little effect in the streambed now filled with NVA regulars. The only outside fire support that could get fire into the streambed was the ARA.

All ARA platoons were alerted and thrust into the fray. Will Pierce first, then me and then 1st Platoon soon after, so that all platoons and all sections were committed. An advance base camp was established at the Tea Plantation, some 20 km from Pleiku and about the same distance from LZ X-Ray. Fuel and ammo were flown in on C-130's that were moving supplies from base camps all over II Corps. Fire mission after fire mission was flown throughout the day and late into the night.

The green-orange tracers of the NVA contrasted with the red tracers of US Forces, giving the ARA a rough picture of the troops deployment.

The sun returned early on the 15th. My first trip was at 06:30.

"Damn. They could at least have waited until after breakfast," I said

"Aw, shut up and eat your crackers," answered Bart, who had only shaved half his face and looked like a *before and after* ad for Gillette.

At LZ X-Ray, the battle was already under way. The NVA were testing their tactics of hugging the enemy. The US Infantry now from both the 1/7 and 2/7 were fighting at extremely close quarters.

"Armed Falcon 66, this is Bonnie Blue 3A. Over," called the Fire Direction Officer of 1/7th.

"3A, this is 66. Over."

"Do you think you can deliver fire within ten meters of our friendlies? Over."

"Can't guarantee there won't be a stray rocket or so, but I think our boys can do it."

"Thanks. We're expecting a real push by the NVA this afternoon and our Intelligence Officer thinks that it will be at real close quarters."

"I expect he's right. What would be good is if you could coordinate the ground based artillery to move their GT line from conflicting with our flight patterns. You wouldn't have to break them off until we were making our runs."

"Roger, 66. I can do that and have the Air Tac Officer move the air support to other targets that won't interfere."

"Sounds good, 3A. Where do you want these rockets?"

"66, just orbit a minute. Sounds like a fire fight is starting on our far left flank."

Ten minutes later, Bart and I had expended our load and were headed back to the Tea Plantation. By 1000 hours, the battle had picked up and, like the day before, each section would shoot, fly back, reload, refuel, take off, fly out, and shoot. All day long this continued.

About 1200 hours, a brigadier general approached me and asked if I thought they were doing any good. I explained that the ARA fires were so desperately needed because of the close range in which the battle was being fought. General Clark, the MACV G4 (the Logistics Officer), said he understood and would bring in rockets from III Corps, because we had already used all the rockets in II Corps.

At 1400 hours, I had reloaded and refueled and was on takeoff when my engine failed. No sweat: an autorotation from 20 feet, so long as you had some airspeed, was not a big deal.

The ground crew attached the wheels and dragged the chopper off the line. A quick check verified what was suspected. The bladders in which the fuel was kept were condensing water which, because water weighs more than JP4 (flight fuel), water was settling in the bottom of the bladder and was being pumped out on the last one or two fuelings. My second attempt to take off resulted in a second autorotation. Bart deserted me and got a fresh bird. Ed Brach joined me. Overall for the day, I had seven engine failures; probably a record.

The battle at LZ X-Ray never paused. Throughout the afternoon, section after section provided very close fire support to the engaged troops.

At 1800 hours, I had finally solved the fuel problem and was dispatched. I was joined by Ed Balda, Dick Washburn and Will Pierce; all three platoons. In all, eight choppers were involved and were streaking toward LZ X-Ray.

"Armed Falcon 64, this is 65 (Charlie Hooks, our Operations Officer). You take the lead and direct the other platoons as needed."

"65, this is 64. Wilco."

"64, this is 62. We're flying echelon just behind you."

"62 and 64, sounds like a plan."

"Armed Falcon 64, this is Bonnie Blue 3A. Over."

"3A, this is 64."

"64, things are very hot here. I have one FO (forward observer) who is really taking heavy fire and needs help. I'm switching you to F2 (fire net 2) so that he can direct your fire mission. Switch now and contact Bonnie Blue 43 A."

"Bonnie Blue 43A, this is Armed Falcon 64. Over."

As soon as 43A opened his mike, I could hear the rattle of heavy gunfire.

"64, this is 43A," came the nervous reply.

"Roger, 43A. I have eight birds. Where do you want their eggs?"

"64, I'm behind a termite mound with our Infantry on the left. Most of the enemy fire is coming from my… (a fresh rattle of machine gun fire)… right… I mean my left, no my it's my right…"

"43A, this is 64. Settle down, we'll get 'em. Face the sun (which was setting), and tell me where the fire is coming from."

"…64, I'm sorry. It's definitely from my left… I mean right."

"43A, are you right-handed?"

"Yes."

"Then face the sun and tell me if the fire is coming from the hand that you use for your fork."

"Roger and thanks. The fire is coming from the right front about 30 yards away. They appear to have climbed trees to get a better angle at us."

43A calmed down and was as cool as the professional soldier he was.

"Okay! I'm going to put a pair of rockets where I believe you're talking about. Adjust my fire so I can bring in the other birds."

"Roger, 64."

"Flight, did you monitor?" A "double click" on the mike confirmed that they had.

I started my run and fired two rockets into a small clump of trees about 30 yards from the termite mound.

"That's it! That's it!"

"Okay, 43A. Flight, we want half a load into those trees. 62, you cover middle out 50 yards. 61, middle in 50 yards. Be careful. No rockets beyond the mound, Okay?"

I led them to the place to begin the rocket run and broke left.

"Go get 'em, 61 and 62."

"Roger that!"

The ships dove and fired 2-4-6-8-10-12-14-16-18 rockets into the area. The rocket motors could be seen bursting apart in the trees and the warheads exploding on the ground. It was a grand sight!

After the final section fired, I assumed lead again.

"43A, this is 64, over."

"Roger, 64. It's so quiet."

"Do you need some more?"

"Negative, 64. Thanks for pulling our tails out of the fire."

"No sweat, 43A. We're going to switch back to F1, just call us if you need us... Bonnie Blue 3A, this is Armed Falcon 64. Over."

"64, this is 3A. We seem to have a lull right now. Thanks for your help."

"Roger, 3A. I'm sending 61 back to reload. 62 and I will remain on station until 61 reports up. Do you want his rockets? He'll have 36 in all."

"64, this is 3A, Roger. Let's put them along our line on the left. Contact Bonnie Blue 66A on F4."

"Wilco, 3A."

Apparently, the NVA (those who were left) moved out later that night. A relief battalion landed in an LZ about two miles from LZ X-Ray and encountered some resistance until they linked up.

Mortar Patrol

Only a week after we had landed and settled in at the Golf Course, we began mortar patrol. As the sun would set, a bird from the 2/20th Artillery would launch and fly over the "Golf Course" until his fuel would run low. Then he'd be relieved by another bird who'd run until his fuel ran low, and after about two hours, his replacement would end the patrol. All night the ARA was on patrol.

Most of the time, *nothing* happened. But occasionally the pilots would spot a VC mortar or a rocket launch and would respond instantly with rocket fire. Generally, that would end the attack and mortar patrol would resume. Thankfully, once your shift was over, your mission was finished for the night, though you weren't relieved from your duties the next day. Well you can imagine how boring it was doing that all night. During the night, the crew would listen to the AFN (Armed Forces Network) and serenade the battalion operations personnel with off key versions of the tunes of the day. Most liked by all was "Folks think I'm big in Detroit City… I want to go home." We'd think longingly about the home we sang of, but there was that big, old Pacific Ocean keeping us here.

One night, Ed Branch, SP4 Gary Pruitt, Sgt. McMahone, and I launched about 10 pm and headed out around the perimeter. At 1500 feet (AGL), it was comfortable about 75°, so we enjoyed our little flight.

About 11 pm, I noticed a cloud bank rolling in about 600 feet (AGL).

"Ed, looks like we got a cloud layer below us. How about you shooting a Ground Control Approach (GCA) to the airstrip."

The GCA radar had only been installed the week before, so no one had much experience with it. The runway lights were small one watt bulbs mounted on sand bags up the right and down the left.

Ed said, "Yeah that would be good."

We headed south and then turned left to 270°.

"Armed Falcon 64, this is Valiant Speaker. The GCA is up and operating. Do you want to shoot an approach?"

"Roger, Valiant Speaker. We're at 2,000 feet, 1200 AGL. Do you have us on your screen?"

"Roger, 64. Affirmative. Continue heading 270°."

"Wilco," I said, indicating that we would comply.

We slowly crept toward the airstrip. At 1500 feet, we entered the cloud bank which I estimated would only be about 25 or 30 feet deep. The voice of the GCA radar guided us as Ed, and I, continued our descent. At 1100 feet, we were still in the clouds and could only see to the windows that enclosed us.

Finally, I said, "Execute a missed approach."

I took controls. The pilot (right seat) only had a magnetic compass, a small artificial horizon, a needle and ball, and a speed indicator (speedometer). I turned to 90° to help the radar operator to capture my image.

"Okay, Ed, keep the racket down so I can execute this approach. I'll probably be leaning on you to pick out your instrument indicators. Bear with me."

Once again, we headed for the airstrip.

The GCA operator was calm and cool.

"You're on center line. Hold it. You're drifting below approach. Slow to 200 feet per minute... I've temporarily lost you due to ground clutter. My assistant confirms that the strip is zero-zero. Continue your approach."

Miraculously, we flew over one of the landing lights. I stopped the chopper at a hover and then moved forward until I saw a second landing light. I gently set the chopper down. We all cheered.

I turned in my seat and asked, "Everyone Okay?"

:Yes, sir," said Ed. "Do you want me to move us off the strip?"

"Yes," I replied.

As soon as he had moved us, I got out and jogged to the GCA shack. We shook hands all around as I thanked them for their help.

The next day, I flew to Pleiku and bought a bottle of scotch for the GCA crew.

Burglary 101

Let's go back to Bart. He was an extraordinary man, a great leader. And he was as cool as a cucumber in all his actions. As we were preparing for Bon Son, Bart decided to add a new twist to our tactics. Bart and I would fly along a road looking to draw fire. When we did, we would fire at the position until the VC gunner would abandon his hole. Our gunner and the crew chiefs would fire covering fire while Bart and I would land and steal the weapon! We collected about fifteen machine guns this way.

Charlie Hooks head about our exploits and convinced Bart to let him fly with me on the next mission that afternoon. Charlie and I bounced about 1330 hours and picked our target road. This road was key to the defense of the VC who dug in around the hamlet of Tam Ky.

Here came the tracers. Orange and green again. We heard only six crumps. I took the controls and selected 4 pairs of rockets. We had lost all altitude and were virtually hovering. I turned right and flew about 100 yards up the road. Charlie grabbed his 40 mm grenade launcher. I U-turned and sped toward the VC's position. Both door gunners fired at the scrambling VC. Finally, he abandoned his position and dove behind a small palm tree. Charlie stuck the 40 mm out the window, aimed, and fired one round. Charlie and I watched in disbelief as the grenade (which you could easily see) curved around the tree and exploded. The VC fell to the ground dead.

It was over.

I landed next to the spider hole and stole his machine gun. Charlie was ecstatic. Even after returning to base camp, it took three days for Charlie to stop smiling.

Yes, dear reader, war is hell. So I am sorry for the gore, but I do want you to understand why this was such a terrible war. In all the preceding wars, both sides had comparable technology: same tanks, same artillery, etc. In Vietnam, we had a giant lead in technology: aircraft, trucks, and on and on. We were the leaders on the technology field. But in Vietnam, we restricted the use of most of our technology because we feared the wrath of the world for beating up on and bullying an inferior force. Our orders followed suit: no bombing along the Main Supply route to the south, the Ho Chi Minh Trail, only restricted bombing in North Vietnam, no flechette rounds, keeping the port of Hai Phong open, and so on. These restrictions and a thousand others effectively tied both of our hands behind our backs.

So we can invent and produce the most sophisticated technology. All the fancy gadgets allowed. But, no matter the foe, we have to develop a new soldier who can deliver on the promise of freedom, economic stability, and security.

Will we ever enter another Vietnam? Never say never. The lesson we should learn is how to configure a military that can respond quickly, define geographic zones, use military force wisely, and can inculcate the leaders of the opposition with thoughts and actions that will enhance freedom stability and security.

General Westmoreland

December slipped by without any major engagements. Christmas was tough. No family, no real bed, no showers, and no Norm. I lightened my load a bit by sending a tape-recorded message to a friend back at Ft. Rucker. This friend called Barbara, my wife, in Little Rock and played the taped message. Barbara was totally surprised and delighted.

Rumors of an infusion made the rounds in January. This infusion would supposedly solve the problem that everyone in the 1st Cav would rotate stateside in the same month. The solution was to replace one half of the division with officers and men from other organizations serving in country.

Bart asked me if I wanted to be infused. I said no thanks, but that was not the end of it. Maj. Bob Evans, who commanded the 120th Aviation Company, at Ton Son Nhut said that the VIP company needed a pilot with an instrument rating.

Bob called me and asked if I would be General Westmoreland's pilot. He promised a bed, warm showers, and good food.

I sought out Bart for advice. Bart and I talked for an hour, after which I decided to take the position.

On March 1, 1965, I reported to the 120th Aviation Company. It was a good assignment. When I wasn't flying Gen. Westmoreland, I was flying Henry Cabot Lodge (the US ambassador to Vietnam) or Prime Minister

Holt of Australia or some visiting dignitary. For a week, I even flew John Wayne and his sidekick, Dom DeLuise. I would pick them up at the Ton Su Nhut helipad and fly them to a secured hamlet near Trang Sup. They would do their scenes for an Army film and later the Green Beret. Promptly at 4 pm, I would pick up Wayne and DeLuise and fly to the Trang Sup Officer's Club. There, they would have a beer and comedian DeLuise would keep us rolling on the floor laughing. The main target of his routine was Dean Martin.

Later, I would fly them to Ton Son Nhut. John Wayne would pose with the soldiers for pictures and autographs. Most days it would last for a couple of hours, but, however long, Wayne and DeLuise would stay until every last solder had their autograph or photograph. Afterwards, they would shower and clean up and meet me at the Officer's club. After dinner, they would return to their rooms and I to mine. John invited me to his home in Santa Monica. Unfortunately, I couldn't leave Vietnam and to go California, but I could dream.

I also regularly flew Westmoreland's Deputy, General Heintges. The first day I flew Gen. Westmoreland was hilarious. The general and his aide flew by L-23 to Cu Chi. The 1st Infantry Division (the Bid Red One) was garrisoned there and General Westmoreland was presenting the Distinguished Service Cross to General DePuy the CG of the division.

My crew and I flew our UH1D (Huey) to meet Gen. Westmoreland and his aide, CPT "Bill" Carpenter – the former Lonesome End of the US Military Academy (USMA) football team. It was Bill's first day as Westmoreland's aide.

When I arrived, I saw Gen. DePuy's aide and Bill frantically searching the ground.

I asked, "What are you looking for?"

Bill replied, "The f------ medal Westmoreland's supposed to present."

I said, "Bill, stand up and search all your pockets."

Bill did, and lo and behold, found the medal in one of his fatigue jacket pockets.

Bill turned and sprinted to the reviewing stand. As he arrived, General Westmoreland received the salute of General DePuy and turned to Bill who coolly gave the medal to Westmoreland, who pinned it on DePuy.

After the ceremony and some pleasantries, Gen. Westmoreland and Bill joined my crew and I, and we departed for Kontum for a command visit. Cu Chi and Kontum are near one another, so our trip was short.

Gen. Westmoreland was smiling as we left, so I knew things went well. The next stop was Song Be.

The crew and I ate a quick lunch. We were just cleaning up when Westmoreland and Bill returned. The General wanted to go to a provisional headquarters about 20 miles from Song Be.

As we approached the camp, a strong monsoonal storm burst over the camp. In the pounding rain, the visibility was zilch.

Three times I attempted an approach and couldn't get in. Finally, I turned to Gen. Westmoreland and said,

"General, it's just too dangerous for us to get in there. I suggest that we try again after our next stop."

Gen. Westmoreland said, "Well I really want to visit there."

I replied, "General, I've got a good record as an aviator, and I don't want to go down in history as the guy who killed the MACV commander."

Westmoreland laughed and said, "You're right, Gene. Let's go to our next stop and then reevaluate."

At the next stop, Tran Quay, it was raining heavily. Gen. Westmoreland asked for his rain jacket. Bill shot me a glare that revealed he hadn't brought it.

I turned around in my seat and handed my jacket to Bill for Gen. Westmoreland. Bill said, "Thanks, Gene. That's twice you've pulled my fat from the fire."

I said, "No sweat! We rookies have to work together."

When Westmoreland and Bill returned to the chopper, General Westmoreland said, "Let's go back to MACV."

I replied, "Yes, sir. But do you want to take another shot at the Provisional Forces (PF) Camp?

"No, Gene, I talked to the CO by radio here at Tran Quay and got the business settled."

They had an uneventful trip to MACV HQS, but I never did get my jacket back.

Among my duties in Ton Son Nhut was being the Administrative Officer for the company. That duty included booking passage for those in the Company who had completed their tour of duty and were returning to the States. It was a rather simple job but could turn and bite you if you weren't careful.

A Sergeant Carter was completing his tour on July 19, 1966.

When I went to book Sergeant Carter's passage, I discovered that he had recently been promoted from E-5 to E-6 and would have to wait receive orders from CONUS for his new assignment.

I telephoned the Pentagon and requested Sergeant Carter's orders be expedited. Finally, the orders arrived on July 24, 1966.

I had booked my own passage for July 25, so I gave up my seat to Sergeant Carter.

The next day, I went to the Saigon Airport with my orders but no seat. I went to the dispatch desk and inquired as to aircraft not transporting troops but cargo that were headed toward the U.S. Sure enough, there was one - a C141 headed for Dover, Delaware, with a couple of stops along the way. I immediately booked passage.

The large cargo hold was nearly full of caskets holding the remains of brave men who had paid the ultimate price. I left the Republic of Vietnam at noon, July 25.

The first stop was Tachikawa AFB in Japan. As the crew and I left the aircraft, one of the pilots noticed some bullet holes in the wing. Therefore, the plane would be grounded until the holes were repaired.

The crew made arrangements for the repairs while I went to the dispatcher to see if I could get another flight. I was extremely lucky in that another C141 was leaving for Travis AFB in California.

I booked passage and left Japan about 8 pm on July 25.

After we were airborne and out over the Pacific, I went forward and met the crew. After the usual chitchat, the pilot asked, "Gene, how would you like to fly this thing for a bit? I've got to take a leak."

I took the controls, turned off the autopilot, and proceeded to make "S" turns. I kept the altitude and airspeed in the proper range and even hooked a compliment from the navigator.

After about half an hour, I returned control to the pilot. It was time to get some rest, but I was way too pumped to get into anything but an "alpha" level sleep, as I dreamed of seeing Barbara and our kids.

In the late afternoon on July 26, we arrived at Travis AFB near San Francisco. I thanked the crew and again sought the dispatcher. It was the middle of the airline strike, and no commercial aircraft were flying east across the Rockies.

A C124 pilot came into the waiting room where I was and announced that he was going to Dallas, Texas. I booked a seat and eventually caught a bus to the flight line. Literally hundreds of transport aircraft were parked on the apron.

As the bus pulled up to the C124, the crew was trying to load a large generator. But because of a stubborn cargo elevator and a not-so-skillful crew, they weren't getting anywhere.

I decided not to risk my future to that crew and retrieved my duffle bag after a short discussion with the loadmaster.

Now I was on the apron with hundreds of cargo planes but no way to get back to operations so that I could book another flight. As I picked up the duffle bag and hoisted it over my shoulder, a pickup truck drove up and the lieutenant driver asked, "Where are you going?"

"Back to the terminal to get a different flight," I answered.

"Toss your bag in the back and I'll take you there."

I was very grateful and the two of us drove to the terminal.

As I walked in, the dispatcher called out that there was a C-141 headed for Dover, Delaware set to depart at midnight. I booked passage and called Barbara.

"Honey, I'm coming home!"

"Where are you now?"

"Travis AFB in California, but I've got a lift to Dover AFB in Delaware."

"When will you get here?"

"I haven't a clue, but why don't you go tomorrow to the Peabody Hotel in Memphis and I'll get there by hook or crook as quickly as I can."

I was thoroughly invigorated. I shaved and cleaned up by changing into wrinkled but at least fresh khakis.

The flight didn't get airborne till after midnight. After we leveled out, I went forward to meet the crew. The crew was the same crew that had taken me from Saigon to Tachikawa. They had gotten their aircraft repaired early the morning after arriving in Japan. Now they were on the way home to Dover.

"Where would you stop if you needed the fuel?" I asked.

"Oh, we won't need to stop for fuel," answered the navigator.

"Ok, I know that," I said, "But where would you stop if you had to?"

Finally the pilot realized that I was trying to get to

someplace short of Dover and said, "Where is your final destination?"

"Memphis, Tennessee," I said.

"That's a bit out of our flight path. How about Kelly AFB in San Antonio, TX?"

"Great."

So at about 9 am, I arrived at Kelly AFB. Again I went to see the dispatcher. There were no flights to Memphis but there was a flight by American Airlines who was defying the strike by flying a route from Houston to San Antonio to Dallas to Memphis, St. Louis, and beyond.

I booked 1st class on that flight to Memphis, which was due to depart San Antonio National in 45 minutes.

With no transportation, I thought it unlikely that I could get there on time since the airport was across town from Kelly, AFB. But then a voice said, "Sir, are you the one who booked a sedan?"

"Yes! Thanks! Let's open the trunk."

I tossed my duffle bag in the trunk and away we sped.

The young airman said, "Where are we going?"

"To the airport I've got a flight to catch."

"I'm not authorized to go off post."

"Let me see your trip ticket."

The airman handed me the ticket, and I signed my name and included my serial number, just in case there was an inquiry.

When we arrived at the airport, I dashed through the terminal to my gate and got there just as the door was closing! Now it was on to Memphis and to my lover/friend/wife. We were at last reunited!

16842
STATES ARMY

STATES

Second Tour

Second Tour

Barbara and I were stationed at Ft. Rucker, Alabama from 1966 to 1968. The living was easy. The most significant thing I did was to write a field manual entitled "Doctrine for the Employment of Attack Helicopters." It outlined the successful tactics that were employed by gunships in Vietnam plus projected those tactics into higher-level conflicts. I considered it a "fun project."

Early in 1968, I received orders back to Vietnam to command C Battery 2/20 Aerial Artillery, the battery I had served with in 1965-66.

In June, I went for five weeks to Hunter AFB to train on the Cobra (AH1G) gunship. When I graduated, Barbara joined me and we spent a lovely second honeymoon on the beaches of St. Simons Island at the Cloister Hotel. The time gave me an opportunity to think about his upcoming command assignment.

One morning, I turned to Barbara and said, "Honey, I've decided that, with the war losing its support here in the US, my mission should be to get no one killed or wounded by enemy action, including myself."

Barbara said, "I like that. We need you to come home in one piece."

"I swear to you, I will."

After the honeymoon, Barbara and I returned to Ft. Rucker where I received the Legion of Merit for my work on the field manual. After our goodbyes, I took the family to Ft. Smith, AR so they could be near family and friends. In late July, I departed for Vietnam.

English

I arrived by C-130 at LZ English on August 1, 1968. When the back door cargo ramp was lowered, it was like standing in front of a blast furnace, only the air was humid and after about ten steps, my fatigues were soaked in sweat.

"Jeez!" I exclaimed. And then to a sweat soaked MP, "Where's the HQs for the 2nd of the 20th ARA?"

"Just straight ahead down this road on the left."

I returned the MP's salute and struggled with my duffle bag down the road to my new boss's office.

"Sir, I'm MAJ Gene Kleese reporting for duty as ordered."

"At ease, Kleese. We're glad to have you aboard."

LTC Franklin had been handpicked for this command. "Let me get a hold of Ed Balda." (Ed was the CO of C Battery and would take over as the S3 when I took command of C Battery.)

"Hey, Sergeant Major, see if you can get a hold of Maj. Balda."

"Yes, sir," came the reply from the adjacent room. "Sit down, Gene."

Franklin was very pointed in his conversation with me. He emphasized that after the battle of Hue, the Army had fought in the battle of Assau Valley. Though the NVA were there, it was hard to pick targets that would have any bearing on winning or losing. After the Assau Valley campaign, the airmobile division (the 1st Cavalry Division) mostly retired to LZ English. Franklin intimated that the retirement was going to end soon. But he said he'd rather not divulge it at this time.

Ed Balda, accompanied by Jim Spears, knocked and entered the office. Both were old friends from the first tour and Ft. Benning. Jim would be my Executive Officer and Ed would be the battalion S3 Operations Officer.

Franklin assigned me to Frank Trevino, the CO of B Battery to help with the opening of a small LZ 15 miles north of English. A typhoon interrupted the plan to move, and Frank and I spent a wet, windy day trying to keep the battery from blowing away. Finally, the storm lifted and the battery moved.

I flew to English after everything was settled. The traditional change of command ceremony was effected in Franklin's office and, just like that, I was a combat leader.

And here we were again. Jim Spears and I walked down the path that led to the helipad.

I said, "How do I get them to bounce?"

Jim replied, "Ring the bell!"

I did and checked my watch. It took ten minutes for the first chopper to lift up.

I told Jim to ring the bell again. This time it took 15 minutes. I was getting hot. The SOP called for a five minute lift off for the first birds and ten minutes for the second section. The third section bounced in fifteen minutes.

"Ring it again!"

Twenty minutes before lift-off! Jim was beside himself.

"Tell them to orbit near the Free Fire Zone at coordinates 770539."

With that, I climbed into an Armed B model HUEY and turned Northwest to intercept my battery.

"Today, we're going to learn how to shoot from 1,500 feet."

And so we went. Every pilot in the battery flew under my perfectionist program.

When the day was done, I called the pilots together. They ate in the mess tent. I then proceeded to remind them that the war was still going on and that they needed to sharpen their skills. I promised that they would practice firing until I was satisfied with their marksmanship. No schedule would be published, and only I and my executive officer, Jim Spears, would know the schedule in advance. I then told Jim that it was my goal to not lose anyone to enemy action—period!!!

Thus the battery was introduced to me, and I was introduced to the battery.

That evening, I asked 1st SGT Smith to assemble all the NCO's at 1700 hours the next day in my tent. I prepared for the meeting by cooling a case of Budweiser.

When the non-com's were assembled, I began the meeting.

"Corporal Ali, how many ammunition men do you supervise?"

"Twelve, sir."

"What is the most serious problem either logistically, operationally, or personnel-wise that you have?"

"My most serious problem is Specialist Greene. He's hung up on marijuana."

I took notes. "Can he be used in any less sensitive area?"

"I don't know, but it's not just Greene. Marijuana is a serious problem. It's like having a bunch of zombies working for you."

"1st SGT, give me your solution."

"Sir, can you let me work for a few days before I answer?"

"Sure, 'Top.' Give me an update by Thursday. Don't worry if it's not all fleshed out, but I want to stop this mess now!"

Now, it was tough. First, you couldn't have everybody ratting on everybody else. Second, you had to get "the facts, ma'am," and not wander around paranoid-bound. And third, the punishment had to fit the crime.

During the first few nights, when Jim and I wandered down the battery's main street in my command, the smell of marijuana would almost make you high. (This was the only exposure I ever had to marijuana.)

Top did a great job in defining the problem, explaining the options, recommending a solution, and developing a program that would supplement the battalion's program. On top of this, I developed a regular program on meeting with the NCO's each week, where we discussed the problems of each and every soldier. This meeting was held every Friday evening at about 1900 hours. I provided the beer or other ordered refreshments, and the NCO's provided me with the deep knowledge of the personnel problems so that they could be handled at the deepest depth.

Morale skyrocketed!

Jim, who was a good athlete, organized basketball, volleyball, and even flag football teams. Everything was going great, but, as I could have guessed, it didn't last long.

Bart's Visit

It was early on a late October morning, before 10 o' clock, and I heard that we were going to have a visitor, but they didn't tell me who, so I just continued doing what I was doing. I was actually talking to one of the maintenance guys about a small technical problem with the helicopters.

I saw the D model HUEY land at our small heliport, and I saw a man get out of the ship and turn and start walking up our stairs toward my office.

"Holy mackerel! That's Bart!" I exclaimed

I ran down the steps to meet him. We hadn't seen each other in a couple of years, but it was a great reunion. I hugged him, and he hugged back with big bear hugs. We walked up and talked about our kids, our wives, and how things were going at home. I congratulated him on making LTC and for taking command of the 101st Aerial Artillery battalion.

He looked great. Same ole Bart, same old crooked grin. He looked confident; he knew where he was going. He didn't stand still at all, he continued to work very, very hard, and everybody knew that, one of these days, he wasn't going to be wearing colonel eagles, he was going to be wearing stars, and, probably before his career was up, and, probably, a lot of them. But, that was not to be.

We went into the mess tent, and we both got some iced tea. We had appropriated an ice machine, and we were very thankful for our precious ice cubes. Where we were at LZ English, by ten, it was hot as blue blazes. I believe it was the hottest place in the whole country. People used to say that hell may be hotter, but not by much. Anyway, we sat down and had our iced tea. Bart and I got to talking about different subjects.

He said, "What's different from when you and I were out there stealing them machine guns and bringing them back to our base?"

"Well, a lot." I said. "Out in the countryside, if you see a machine gun or if someone is shooting at you, you can just about bet your bottom dollar that there are four more that can fire support for the original machine gun emplacement. You have to be very, very careful if you were going to conduct a battle damage assessment (BDA), so just be aware of that and don't expose yourself to that type of fire. Don't expect to be able to go down there and pick up the machine gun because that would be deadly."

We went on to other subjects until early afternoon, and he said, "I have to get back."

I told him, "You're welcome to come over and see me anytime. Maybe we can be a little more formal. Next time I'll try to get something prepared for us."

"Well you take care of C Battery, it's my Battery."

"It's our battery."

The truth is both he and I left our fingerprints all over C Battery.

With that, he left and went back to his helicopter. And away he flew.

About a month later, I got word that Bart had been shooting at a machine gun emplacement near Da Nang. He had the division artillery commander, Colonel Vogel with him. They had fired on a machine gun and went down to get a BDA, and he was shot down. It killed Bart, it killed Colonel Vogel, and it killed his co-pilot and both crew members. It was tragic.

Bart's potential was wiped out. I wish he had taken my comments more seriously, but I guess if wishes were horses, all beggars would ride.

Shortly after Bart's visit, the Battalion Commander called for a meeting. "Gene – Franklin."

"Yes, Sir!"

"Come up here now (if you can)."

"Yes, Sir."

I jogged quickly up the hill.

"Sergeant Major."

"Yes, Sir. Boss wants you now."

I knocked on Franklin's door. "Come in, Gene."

"Major Kleese reports as directed."

"Jeez, Kleese, sit down. What do you think of your battery?"

"We're good, but a little immature."

"Can you handle an independent assignment to the Central Highlands?"

"Yes, sir! I have concentrated on making our battery battle-ready, and, while we're not completely ready, we're close enough."

"Okay! Here is your mission: C Battery will be attached to the 1st Brigade of the 1st Cav. You will provide artillery support – either direct, general support, or reinforcing support. You will base at Kontum near the 27th Arty and 1st Brigade HQ. Departure will be by 10-29-68. (In two days.)"

When I left LTC Franklin, I went to my command post and called the 1st SGT; Jim, my XO; and Frank Zapata, my Operation Officer. I appointed Jim to be in charge of the move. He did a great job and had the battery up and ready to fight 24 hours ahead of schedule.

Okay! It was fun. Independent, in charge, able to maximize the battery's combat power…

Six weeks after we arrived at Kontum, the cobras arrived: AH1Gs. They were great. These birds had twice the firepower, twice the maneuverability, and twice the ease of flying. Those of us in C Battery processed in all of the battalion's cobras so that, at one time, we had 12 UH1C's (with armament) and 24 cobras. The battalion picked up 12 cobras, but not for a month. So for a good while, we had 36 gunships. A super Aerial Rocket Artillery Battery.

Grounded Birds

About two months after I settled my battery in Kontum, Jim Spears; Chuck Palmer, my maintenance officer; and I sat in the mess-hall at about 1600 hours to answer that age old question—"to fly or not to fly?" The brigade to which my battery and I were attached was planning to make a Brigade size airmobile operation east of Song Be at 0630 hours the next morning. Every ounce of energy was poured into making this operation a big success. I had been working diligently for almost a month and had sustained a 90% availability rate for almost three weeks in a row. But my parade was about to be rained upon.

Back stateside, magna flux imaging had detected small cracks in the tail rotor cuffs of the cobras. This meant that all cobra helicopter tail rotor cuffs were to be magna fluxed before they could fly again. That evening, I dispatched two cobras and Maintenance Officer Chuck Palmer to the 632nd Maintenance Battalion. There, Chuck could expedite the magna flux operation of our cobras.

Before he left, Chuck gave Jim Spears and I a detailed briefing on how to use dye check to detect cracks in the rotor cuffs. We worked throughout the night to dye check all 10 cobras.

Thankfully, no cracks were detected.

I dispatched a complete platoon of cobras to Song Be and held the other seven birds in reserve. All of the

Brigade Landing Zones were cold (meaning that the lead choppers had not encountered enemy fire).

I ordered two more choppers to the Maintenance Battalion. When I received news that the first two helicopters dispatched last night were returning, I re-routed them to Song Be.

I had the second of the two helicopters pick me up at the Kontum battery location and fly to Song Be. Only very light resistance had been encountered by the brigade, so the entire operation took on the look of a brigade training exercise.

"Big Thunder six. This is Armed Falcon 66. Over." (Big Thunder Six was the Brigade Commander.)

"Armed Falcon 66 this is Big Thunder 6. Over."

"Roger, 6. I just wanted to inform you that we have six birds at Sierra Bravo's, and on top of that, we have four birds operational at Kontum."

"66 this is 6. Over. I'm going to call this thing off. At least we have demonstrated that we can project our combat power anywhere in the III Corps region."

"Thanks, 6. I'll see you back in base camp."

With that, the exercise was wound down.

The Purple Heart?

My tour was half past. LTC Schnibben, our new Battalion Commander, called me and informed me that I was to go on R&R in Hawaii and that I should transition C Battery to Jim Hinton, who had replaced Jim Spears as my XO.

Jim and I worked ourselves through a 100% inventory of all the battery's supplies and equipment in just two days! Now, it was only three days before I was to go on R&R.

On the first day I moved from Kontum down to Phouc Vinh. On the second day, Ed Balda and I transitioned the S3 position.

After all the chaos, I was tired, so I turned in early. I had wonderful dreams of my wife, Barbara, and couldn't wait for that last day to start.

Suddenly, enemy rockets fell in the middle of the compound. I leapt from bed, grabbed my boots, and sprinted toward the TOC.

I made it halfway and encountered a row of unforgiving pallets that were being used to bridge across the temporary lake that had formed during the last monsoonal shower. In full sprint mode, I connected with the pallets and fell ass over teacups into the muddy lake. I arose and limped slowly into the TOC. There I was greeted by my soon-to-be Operations Sergeant, SGT Wilson.

"What happened to you?" SGT Wilson asked.

"I tripped over those damn pallets. I think I broke my big toe," I said through gritted teeth. A medic appeared, almost magically, and examined the now swollen metatarsal.

"It's for sure broken," pronounced the medic. "I've got to fill out this form so they can award you a Purple Heart.

"I don't want a medal for tripping over a ##@#$ pallet. Now go out there and find someone who's really hurt. Sarge, how about sending someone over to my hooch and fetch me a clean set of fatigues?"

The rockets had ceased falling and the new day was being gloriously revealed by its artist.

I had a big day planned, and it all pointed to 1500 hours when my plane would leave Vietnam for Hawaii. My first task would be to secure a chopper and fly to Vung Tau to visit the PX there. I hoped to find a pair of sneakers that I could cut out the top and rest my mangled toe. It only took 30 minutes to find a shoe that would suffice. I also picked up a present for my wife, a beautiful diamond ring. She would fuss but in all honesty, love it.

I was back in Phouc Vinh by lunch, and I joined LTC Schnibben and Ed Balda. I couldn't stop looking at my watch. Finally, at 1430 hours, I caught my chopper, flew to Ton Son Nhut, boarded my R&R bird, and flew to Hawaii.

Barbara met me at the airport and the two of us spent five grand holidays on the beaches of Oahu. I won't bore you with the details, but let's just say that I returned to Vietnam refreshed and invigorated.

Now, that I was back, I faced new challenges. As I entered the compound, I sensed that something just wasn't right. Some of the men in the TOC seemed to want to talk to me but would withdraw before I could find out what was buggin' them.

I found SGT Wilson, my Operations SGT, "Wilson, what the hell is going on?" I asked.

"Nothing much" said SGT Wilson, "but I think you ought to talk to LTC Schnibben so that he can brief you on all the things that went on this week."

"Thanks, Sarge."

I left the TOC and headed for LTC Schnibben's office.

"Hey Sergeant Major is your boss in?" I asked the senior non-commissioned officer of the command.

"Yes sir. Do you want me to get him down here?"

"Please," I answered.

The CSM swiveled at his desk and picked up the PA microphone. "Attention LTC Schnibben, attention LTC Schnibben. Please return to your office; Major Kleese is waiting for you." His voice rang throughout the compound.

"Hey SMAJ, that's straight out of 'No Time for Sergeants'," I laughed. "The next thing you'll want, is for us to call you Gomer!"

"What the hell is so funny, Sergeant Major?" asked LTC Schnibben as he entered the office.

"Maj. Kleese was just admiring our PA system," said the CSM with a twinkle in his eye. "You'll notice that the power resides in whoever controls the microphone, and that would be me."

LTC Schnibben and I just laughed.

"Gene, I'm glad that you had such a great R&R, but, I have to be the bearer of some bad news," said Schnibben staring at the ground between his feet. "Gene, didn't you brief me on your policy that the revetments could only be stocked with no more than a half-a-load of ready rockets?"

"Yes sir. And, I briefed Major Hinton specifically on that policy, because we were having a dialogue with the Ammunition SGT; SGT Taylor, who thought that the whole thing was a make-work policy. So, what happened?" I asked, fearing the worst.

"Well, Jim told me that you had briefed him, but he let SGT Taylor and your ammunition crew rule the day and put about 100 rockets in each revetment. Last Friday, the VC launched a rocket attack that zeroed in on those revetments and the Cobras nearby. One of their rockets scored a direct hit on the cobra parked in the next to the last revetment and its explosion set off each revetment in turn. Every structure that was above ground was ripped apart and blown away including your old hooch, the mess-hall and the trailer that held your after work break room."

"Were there any casualties?" I asked, looking for a miracle.

"None. And when you go there to visit, you'll wonder how."

I put my hands together and thanked my maker. "Well sir, I'd like to make that trip right now. Is our D model up?"

"Yeah, go ahead. But don't be too harsh on Jim. I've already extracted my pound of flesh."

"Yes Sir. I'll keep that in mind."

As I neared Kontum, I kept thinking about how lucky and/or blessed we were that no one was killed. I couldn't believe the odds.

Jim Hinton was contrite and apologetic. I knew that he would make a good commander of C Battery; our discussion that afternoon had more to do about having to sit down and make the tough decisions even though it might be unpopular. Jim promised to do just that. I left shortly after we finished the tour of the battery. I'd seen SGT Taylor but did not speak to him.

Tet '69

It was February, and business was slow. The officers were back to letting the pilot's dictate their own training. I had talked to LTC Schnibben about that, and he agreed that the officers should be using the down time to sharpen their skills.

I left the TOC about 1700 hours. I consumed a good A ration meal and went to my hooch to get some rest.

I had just closed my eyes when SGT Wilson came into my hooch and said, "Sir, it's getting kinda hot. Think you better come over."

I grabbed my fatigues, put on my boots, and walked across the compound.

It was busy in the TOC, but I gathered all the necessary information involving the emerging Tet '69 operation. I made my biggest mistake right then. I failed to wake up LTC Schnibben.

Throughout the night, I routed cobras from one end of III Corps to the other. At one time, I had twenty-two birds in the air, but, each time I ran short of birds, two more would come up to fire their mission. Finally, about 0630 hours, it all shut down.

I contacted the battery commanders and congratulated them on fighting the biggest battle for ARA, during this tour.

I stepped out of the TOC and immediately encountered LTC Schnibben. Schnibben was shaving out of his helmet, but that didn't deter him from extracting his pound of flesh. LTC Schnibben finished his chewing out with a reminder to me that HE was the battalion commander, not me.

The next night, the TET offensive continued. There were still attacks on the main cities by the NVA, particularly north of Hue, and we were busy, but not nearly as busy as we were the first night, but believe me, I made certain to grab LTC Schnibben awake prior to the launch of the first helicopter team fire mission.

He came in the TOC while I was there. I swear he didn't say a word. He didn't interrupt me at all. He stood there and watched me do the insert and, after the battle was over at about 0430 hours, things seemed to calm down, and we handed it back off to the Battery commanders, and they took control again.

On the third night, I don't recall getting any fire missions like we'd had the first two nights, so the TOC operations reverted almost naturally to the stand down posture. That sort of wrapped up our TET '69. It was not as traumatic as it was for the people being attacked. I'm sure the people in Ton Se Nhut had a heck of a tougher night than we did up there in our LZ.

The Sikorsky Visit

I had a routine. Just as brushing my teeth and shaving in the morning, after lunch I would go on my midday stroll. Inevitably, it would wind up on the flight line where I would BS with the crew chiefs and mechanics as they cared for their precious war machines. Their work was hot, dusty, dirty, and hard. But the birds were put together well at the Ft. Worth bell Helicopter plant, so unexplainable mechanical problems were rare.

This particular day in mid-April was a bit out of the ordinary. I watched two men dressed in short sleeved Hawaiian shirts and carrying briefcases approach the flight line. The first thing that popped into my mind was *why weren't these men in their uniforms?* Thankfully, my verbal remarks were more courteous than my initial thoughts.

"How can I help you?" I asked the two.

"Are you Major Kleese?" said the first.

"Yes, sir, in the flesh."

"Well, we'd like to ask a few questions of you."

"Sure. Are you Viet Cong spies?" I kidded.

"No. Not hardly. We're engineers from Sikorsky. We've determined that you have the most flying hours in the Cobra as anyone in or out of the country."

"Huh," I grunted. "I'll be darned."

"My name is Jim Faille, and my partner here is David Goldstein.

We all shook hands. David opened his briefcase and pulled out a form. Jim said, "Give me your impression of the Cobra, Gene.

"Sure. It's a quantum leap from the jerry-rigged HU1B's or C's we were flying. It's faster, more maneuverable, and reliable."

"So, you like it," Jim added

"Sure, what's not to like?" I asked.

"What are the strongest and weakest points?" Jim said.

"Well, the strongest are those that I said… faster, more maneuverability, etc., and the two greatest failures that, in my mind, leave unnecessary vulnerabilities are the facts that it still sports a tail rotor and that you can't move out of your seat to help or perform first aid on your pilot or co-pilot."

"What do you mean?" said Jim.

"Well, let me tell you a story."

It had been nearly four months since this happened. The men moved from LZ English down to their new base camp just north of where they were now in Kontum. There was a Special Forces camp, a fairly large one, in the area that they called the Parrott's Beak. It was so named for the salient that the Laos border makes into what you would think would be Vietnamese territory. The VC and the NVA used it as a drop off point for the Ho Chi Minh trail. Hundreds of tons of equipment and food and ammunition were dumped there and distributed to all the VC units south. One can see why both the US army and the VC thought that control of this area was key. This piece of territory was fought over again and again, probably even by the French who went before the Americans. Well, this time the US got called out to go and protect the base that was under attack. It turned out to be a very hair-raising experience.

Joel Shultz was flying wing. Barry Knowl was his air craft commander. Everything looked swell. I had gone up on top to watch the show. Everything looked like it was going to be routine.

You must understand that, when you respond to a fire mission, you're assumed to have pre-flighted the aircraft before your launch. Unfortunately, neither Joel nor his air craft commander had conducted a pre-flight inspection. Unbeknownst to them, there was one teeny weenie problem. The eye bolt that anchored the left side rocket tubes failed and the rockets pointed up in the air so that, when the fire button was thumbed, the rockets launched at an angle of nearly 45° and hit one of the main rotor blades.

Joel screamed over the radio, "I shot off one of my rotors. I'm going in."

Over the radio, I called Joel and told him to auto rotate and to go for a landing on top of the Special Forces camp.

His ship was gyrating in a big elliptical circle as he fell from about 1,200 feet. Everyone shut up as they watched the climax. I descended and turned on my landing light to light an area for Joel to shoot for. In seconds, he was on the ground. His bird was totaled, but no one was hurt seriously.

The next morning, I arranged for a Chinook to move the helicopter down to the 620th Maintenance Battalion to see what they could salvage, but it was pretty well bent up.

I recommended Joel and his co-pilot be awarded the Distinguished Flying Cross. Although Joel had destroyed about 6 feet of the rotor, the spar tube (the tube that runs down the length of each blade) was not broken. How come? I couldn't say. I was just glad to have Joel and Barry back.

Jim exclaimed, "Holy cow! That's an incredible story!"

I made a jocular comment. "I tell 'em like I see 'em."

Tomorrow

It was only a few days away. And I was ready. All my combat gear had been turned into supply, including my .45 automatic. I had said all my good byes. I had shaken hands with everyone in the 2/20th ARA Headquarters area at least twice. Now it was time to go. I was then transferred to a holding company in Ton Son Nhut.

The next day I was summoned by the commander of the holding company, MAJ Tom Watson.

"Kleese, come up here to my office," MAJ Watson said over my phone.

"I'll be right up," I replied.

Probably a second good-bye party, I thought. Oh well.

I knocked on Tom's door.

"Come in, Gene," Tom said. "Sit down, Gene. Last night, we had a serious accident. A Huey was downed by "friendly fire." It was apparently hit by 155 Artillery fire, and we need to go out there and find it, recover the bodies, and prepare for the aircraft to be hauled out by Chinook."

"Tom, I'd really like to help, but, you know, I'm going home tomorrow, and, what's more, I've turned in all my gear. I really am sorry."

"You can use my gear, even my pistol. And I'll throw in a clean set of jungle fatigues."

"Okay! Okay! I'll go," I said. "Can you gather up some grunts and a few weapons? Maybe a 60mm mortar and a couple of M60's?"

"Sure, we have an infantry squad ready to launch and we've already loaded the M60's, and a mortar shouldn't be a problem, right, SGT Sanchez?"

"No, sir," said Sanchez who had been standing across the room and had gone unnoticed till now.

Tom said, "Gene, this is SGT Sanchez, and he'll be the squad leader."

We shook hands. The strength of his grip was reassuring.

"Anything else, Gene?" Tom asked.

"No. Let's meet at the heliport at 1000 hours," I said.

SGT Sanchez affirmed. "Sounds good, Major Kleese. Okay, MAJ Watson?"

"Sure," responded Tom.

And our meeting broke up.

At precisely 1000 hours, I walked on the helipad toward the "D" model Huey. The infantry squad stood at attention just in front of the Huey.

I asked, "Does everybody have three canteens of water?"

In unison, they replied, "Yes, sir!"

"Okay, let's load up."

I went to the left side of the Huey and introduced myself to the pilot, aircraft commander, and the crew chief. I told them not to fire suppressive fires on the LZ, or anywhere else for that matter. There had been no VC action in the area for over a year, and I didn't want to wake up any of them. They nodded, and I took my seat.

"Fire in the hole," the AC said.

And the blades started to rotate.

A short 20 minute flight took us to the LZ, and our approach took us to the northeastern portion of the LZ. I told the AC to orbit until we landed and confirmed that the LZ was cold.

"Wilco," said the AC as he landed through elephant grass that was at least 10 feet tall.

Out of the chopper came the infantry squad, SGT Sanchez, and myself. SGT Sanchez used his compass for orientation while the squad organized in a diamond formation. We moved to the Northeast into a triple canopy jungle. The temperature jumped to at least 110° F. The air was hot to the lungs. I quickly went through the first canteen and started on the second.

After a half mile, we came upon the crash scene. The Huey was almost on the ground and was tilted forward. The tail was intact and pointed to the sky. The two dead pilots were in their seats and a 155 artillery shell was imbedded in the transmission, unexploded.

I had the squad back away to 25 yards, just in case the round exploded. Also, I limited the umber of people who could be in the 25 yards blast zone to two personnel. I called base and told them to get EOD to defuse the shell.

The squad recovered the two bodies and placed them in body bags. We opened a stretcher and hauled the two men back to the LZ.

I called AC in the chopper who had inserted us, and we set up a perimeter as the helicopter landed. Back to Ton Son Nhut in 20 minutes, and mission accomplished!

Back to tomorrow!

Leaving Vietnam

It was late July, hot and dry, but I was going home. This time, my trip would be easier than the first time.

I made a special trip to the batteries and shook their hands and thanked them for all their support. I also spoke to all the enlisted personnel to thank them especially for their hard work and long hours.

Then, on August the 12th, I joined the going home soldiers and flew to Travis AFB in California and subsequently through Little Rock to Ft. Smith, Arkansas.

I caught a cab from the airport to Barbara's house and arrived just after midnight. The kids were excited as were both Barbara and I.

My first words to Barbara were. "See? I didn't even get a scratch. And no one in my command was wounded or killed."

As the war progressed, it was painfully evident that the US citizenry were increasingly tired of sending their sons as drafted soldiers to fight and to die in the strange, far away land of Vietnam. From the arrival of the 1st Cavalry Division in 1965 until the evacuation of the embassy in 1974, for ten years we followed a flawed strategy. It was too much for our soldiers, too much for the weary US citizens at home, too much for the South Vietnamese, the soldiers, and their leaders. We were whipped, and we quit the field. How does a soldier respond?

My father was a soldier in WWII who fought in the Pacific. He retired as a Lieutenant Colonel. His two sons were soldiers. Both of us fought two tours in Vietnam and retired as LTC's.

My son was a soldier and retired in 2004 as a Major. All of us men served our country. All of us loved our country (right or wrong). All of us enjoyed serving. But we didn't dodge the draft, throw our medals on the White House lawn, or pose in control of an enemy air defense artillery gun. Even as we sit here today, we would serve wherever the Army would send us, now or in the future.

So, dear friends, You know a little about me for now. As back ground and out of gratitude for his raising me and my siblings I'd like to present a special story about my father.

Hobo Jim

A fictional story inspired by the adventures of James G. Kleese, LTC U.S. Army

Gene Kleese

Edited by Lindsay McKissick

Hobo Jim

May 4, 1916

Spring had only whispered its presence in the prime dairy farmland of Wisconsin. The rich soil already supported the growth of dark green grass that stretched from horizon to horizon. Sentinel-like farm houses seemed oddly out of place in the otherwise un-dramatic terrain. A light frost blanketed the scene this morning, and in the pre-dawn light, the cows announced their need to be milked and tended. Jim was running away from home. Only twelve, but he thought of himself as a man, not a boy, and he could no longer abide by the conditions that prevailed a barely half mile behind. His mother had died and his father was a drunk. He had been foisted off on his grandmother, Madiline, along with his older sister Helen and his younger brother Jack. Though he had truly tried, he could not find the love his mother had provided either from his grandmother, who, quite openly, hated all men, or from his father, when he was sober.

And Jim was not particularly loving either. Though not mean, he couldn't resist playing practical jokes. Since he was very clever, these jokes normally worked very well. Exasperation could have been his middle name. His sister, on a freezing February morning, had been his latest victim of a practical joke when he enticed her to "taste" the iron pump handle. With the jerk of her head, she left a sizable piece of her tongue behind. The beating administered by his grandmother for that incident was brutal. She took great pleasure in watching Jim wince in pain from the blows of her whipping stick, which was a four foot long steel rod. Subsequent beatings were even crueler as these were delivered for crimes both real and imagined. By May, Jim had had enough.

He had come to the fork. Left would take him back to Colby, the small farming town where he could find work and shelter from sympathetic folks who "understood." Right would take him toward the railroad tracks that led southwest to La Crosse and beyond.

He turned right as he heard the whistle of the morning freight as it climbed Setlers Hill. He ran toward the tracks and arrived just as the engine crossed the intersection, its light cutting through the still dark morning pointed southwest, giving Jim the hope and promise that a better future lay beyond the horizon away from Colby, away from his grandmother and father and away from the blanket of sympathy that could suffocate his free soul.

His young legs carried him easily at the pace of the freight and he had no problem swinging himself into an apparently empty boxcar, his small knapsack preceding. Jim's eyes slowly adjusted to the gloom. He saw that he wasn't alone. Two men, one black and one white, sat in opposite corners in the front end of the boxcar.

The white man growled, "Hey boy! What do you got in that bag?"

"None of your business" said Jim, lowering the pitch of his voice as far as he could.

"Boy, you don't know just what old Jack's business is" said the man as he rose to his feet.

He wasn't big, about five foot five, but Jim could make out the awful mean flat features of the man's face. He was dirty and he stunk. Of one thing Jim was sure, this man was the ugliest, meanest man he had ever seen. Jim took a step backwards.

The young, black man still seated said, "C'mon, Mean Jack, leave him alone."

Mean Jack quickly turned toward the black and snapped, " Nigger, you'd best shut your black ass up tight unless you want this shiv to get acquainted with your liver."

Even in the dim light, the shine of the blade was unmistakable. The black mumbled something Jim couldn't make out, but whatever it was seemed to satisfy Mean Jack so that he could concentrate on Jim without interference.

Jim continued to retreat towards the back of the boxcar nearly

tripping over a one by four lying on the floor. As Mean Jack advanced, Jim picked up the board. A cold sweat trickled down the nape of Jim's neck as he griped the board. He sensed that if he couldn't make his first blow decisive, he'd never get a second. Now Mean Jack was intent on teaching this young brat a real lesson. He was good with a knife and had amply earned his reputation in the hobo camps from Texas to Manitoba.

"Hey boy, drop that board before it gives you a splinter." Jack laughed at his own poor joke. Jim continued to retreat but this time toward the open door from whence just an eternity ago, he had come. Scared, but not paralyzed, he figured that if his single blow didn't connect, at least he might be able to escape out into the Wisconsin dawn.

"Gawd dammit, boy! I said 'drop that board!" Jack slowly tossed his knife from hand-to-hand and continued his menacing advance. Jim's voice fairly trembling, squeaked "You bastard! stay away from me or I'll bash your head in."

Jack laughed, "Jeeze! Just listen . . ."Jim saw his opening and swung - hard! Bulls eye! The board struck paydirt in the groin. .Jack's surprised look lasted only an instant as he doubled over in agony. Quick as greased lightning, Jim ducked behind the moaning figure and with the strength that only fear and adrenalin can engender, shoved the wounded bum out the door. He watched as Jack tumbled down a slope and was quite frankly relieved when he saw the battered figure struggling in vain to stand. At least he was alive.

The freight roared off in the morning early light. "Hot damn!" came a voice from beside him. Jim nearly jumped out the door himself. He had completely forgotten the black man.. "You done whupped Mean Jack. Wait till they hear about that! Hot damn!" The black man's voice assured Jim that there had been but one threat. "What's your name, boy?" the black man was only about eighteen, but the mileage he had accrued made him appear and act much older. Jim took no offense at being called "boy" by this black man only five or six years his senior.

He was still shaking from the excitement of battle but answered "Jim, what's yours?"

"Jim, I'm Gabe. Gabriel Peters. Pleased to make your acquaintance." He stuck out his big paw, and the warmth of that handshake bound the two for a lifetime friendship.

September 15, 1920

Hot!. Hot was the operative word. The sun was hot, the wind was hot, the metal on the thrasher was hot, the fire in the boiler was hot, and the door that he had to open continuously to stuff the straw (fuel) was double hot. Jim had grown. He measured an inch over six feet, and his broad shoulders accentuated his narrow hips and amply muscled frame. He was a good worker and Gabe and he had no trouble finding work during the summer wheat harvest season. Each year they had followed the harvest from Oklahoma to Manitoba. From June to September, the rolling plains of America's breadbasket yielded their golden grain to men and machines toiling beneath the relentless sun. Where was it hotter? For sure not in hell, they said. The men lived mainly in hobo camps and not on the farms they worked. Each camp had its own social structure - pecking order and if you knew where you stood, generally you could keep out of trouble. Thievery, surprisingly, was not a problem, but then they had very little to steal - a bedroll, a knapsack and maybe a souvenir. At night, they would cook their supper over one of the numerous campfires, drink little applejack and tell tales. These were not bums. They didn't beg, except for work. They were independent and liked the life of a rover rather than the responsibilities that would inevitably come with a more settled life.

Jim had learned from Gabe, and Gabe had learned from Jim. Jim had learned survival. Gabe, in the early years, taught Jim how to be a successful hobo. How to ride the rails, how to find work, how to protect what you had, how to sleep with one eye open, how to cook a rabbit on a spit and a thousand other skills only the hoboes knew. Jim taught Gabe how to read, how to write, how to do figures; and how to do math puzzles. Through constant practice, Jim was a master of the latter. How he loved to brag on those puzzles he solved. While he only had an eighth grade education, no one would deny that he could run circles around most who had high school diplomas. Some of the more perceptive farmers had recently let Jim help them with their books. Jim also was getting to be a good mechanic. His father, when sober, had worked in a garage, and Jim had handed wrenches, screwdrivers, and pliers to assist. He had more than a basic understanding of how things worked.

Mean Jack had survived. It was said he'd sworn to open Jim up like an orange if they met again. Fortunately, hobo news traveled faster than the telegraph, and Gabe and Jim always seemed to know which camps to avoid. Perhaps this day the lines had melted. This had been the last day of the harvest in Manitoba, and it had been unusually hot and unusually long. Four times Jim had used baling wire, chewing gum, and swear words to patch the thrasher together. Gabe just laughed. Red faced, Jim would swear at Gabe, but Gabe just laughed louder. In camp, they arrived late. Gabe, who could take the heat better than Jim, was the more refreshed. Jim tired, still hot and not in the greatest of moods, could think of nothing but rabbit stew, applejack, and a well earned rest on his bedroll.

Gabe sensed it first. "Jim, somtin's not right."

The camp's many fires shed ample light on the scene.

"Jeeze, Gabe, leave me be. All I want is to grab some stew, jack, and shuteye," Jim groaned.

"No! Now look at how everybody's watchin'. Something ain't right." Gabe's instincts were on alert twenty four hours a day.

"Dammit, Gabe! You're always imag…." He didn't get the last words out as he had spotted a smallish man with a flat mean face. Though it had been dark that Wisconsin pre-dawn, Jim instantly knew that he again was looking at Mean Jack. A cigarette butt hung from the slash that served as a mouth, and the scar that ran from under the left eye to the bulb of his nose accentuated his ugliness. A crumpled grey hat sat perched on his greasy unkempt hair, and his filthy undershirt covered his undeveloped frame. While most hoboes worked either on farms harvesting or on odd jobs in town, Mean Jack merely intimidated. He was a bum. And a dangerous bum at that. There were dead hoboes buried in shallow graves up and down the heartland put there by Mean Jack's knife.

"Well, if it ain't my good friend and his nigger," sneered Jack drawing his knife from its belt scabbard. "I think I owe you a *bon voyage* on a rail to hell."

" Look friend, I'm tired and not interested in going anywhere," Jim answered. "Why don't you put your knife away before you cut yourself."

From behind, two of Jack's cohorts pinned Gabe's arms as Jack moved to attack his unarmed prey. Though Jim moved quickly, the knife slashed his left arm bringing crimson blood and stinging pain. His choices were limited. He could run and leave Gabe, but he knew Gabe wouldn't last three seconds. He had to fight. What's more, he had to finish the fight so there would be no future threat.

How many of those hoboes resting in their graves had faced similar choices, Jim wondered?

Mean Jack pressed the attack, expertly thrusting and slashing. Jim dove to the ground rolling, grabbing a burning limb from the nearby campfire and bouncing to his feet. All of this action was completed so quickly and athletically that even Jim was surprised! Fear could do marvelous things! Now, Jack's back was to the fire, and Jim, facing him, brandished his weapon and hoped he appeared to be dangerous. Jack stepped back. Too close to the fire, he tried to side step, but Jim cut him off and feigned with the burning torch. Suddenly, Jack's pant leg caught afire. He screamed in pain and began to run. His knife, Jim, Gabe, and the whole world forgotten, he panicked and ran fanning the flames. "Oh, Gawd! Oh, Gawd! Oh, Gawd!" The fire leapt higher and higher and began to engulf him. As he stumbled and fell still screaming most of the hoboes turned away from the horrible scene. It was over. When they finally could get close enough to turn him over, Jack was dead. The two bums who had held Gabe's arms had fled. Jim was confused. On one hand, he wanted to coax life back into the charred body that lay still before him but on the other hand he was relieved that he would never again be threatened by the mean soul of the man he had killed. Jim discarded his torch and knelt on one knee beside the corpse.

Gabe whispered in his ear, "Jim, let's get out of here before the police arrive. They certain to hear that scream and they'll lock you up tight for sure."

A cool breeze began to blow as they left the camp. A short walk brought them to the railyards and a freight headed southeast took them to a haven in the northern woods of Minnesota. As was their custom, each year they became lumberjacks in the winter. Only this year, they'd be a bit early.

January 14, 1921

Bitter, bitter, bitter cold. The slightest breeze knocked frozen limbs off the tall white pines like icicles. Their loud report sounded like gunfire on a not so distant battlefield. A steady snow filtered to the forest floor through a canopy of intertwined branches and pine needles far above. The snow was too dry to cling for long to the branches and even the imperceptible sway of the trees brought whiffs of powder to the ground below. The northern woods seemed endless. Small frozen lakes with their small frozen rivers made passage possible in winter. The timber had to be harvested then, for the boggy terrain was impassible during the spring and early summer. Jim and Gabe had found work in a lumber camp well run by a strict Norwegian named Volkmar. Gabe was the cook, and Jim was an axeman. The day began well before dawn with a big breakfast. Gabe threw his heart into this meal for it was the last before supper that the crews would normally eat. The men loved Gabe's cooking and bragged he was the best in the northern woods. Actually, anything hot in the morning tasted like Waldorf's finest. Where Jim hated the heat, Gabe hated the
cold. That cold more than his love of cooking, motivated Gabe to be at his best in the warm kitchen rather than behind some axe in the frigid forest.

Like most mornings, the crews were organized and in the woods at dawn, Their stomachs full and ready for a full day's work. This day it was Jim's turn at the sled. The axemen rotated this difficult task. It meant harnessing the camp mule, Bunyon, to a lumber sled, going from crew to crew and with their assistance loading their harvest for the trip to the lake. There he would have to unload the lumber alone with a long pike and roll it on to the ice. This work would go on until sunset. It was Jim's last trip. Bunyon, his ears pinned back and his front legs braced, was going no farther. He refused to pull this load of logs another inch. Though only four in the afternoon light was beginning to fade. The grey slate sky had shed its flakes all day.

"Dammit to hell, Bunyon! We're on the last load and its only half a mile to the lake and most of that's downhill. Now git!" Jim gave the leads another vigorous tug. Bunyon just bared his teeth.

"No kickee the mule!" the Chinese head mule skinner had ordered. But by God this time was an exception. Jim hauled off and booted Bunyon in the flank as hard as he could. Bunyon just grunted. Desperate, Jim got an idea. "By God, I'll move your ass." Gathering fallen boughs, branches and twigs, Jim built a pile beneath Bunyon's belly, and through vigorous fanning, finally got a fire started. At first Bunyon, just stood there. Suddenly, his ears flicked forward and squealing he took five steps forward… enough to pull the sled directly over the now blazing fire. There he stopped with renewed resolve to go no farther. Jim cursed and pulled to no avail. He begged Bunyon to move. All of his efforts failed and the sled caught fire. Now Bunyon began to scream and to move. Jim had no choice but to cut him loose and let the sled and logs burn. Bunyon trotted off toward his stables.

Now, Jim had a choice. He could return to camp and face Volkmar's wrath, or he could take off and leave camp. It wasn't a hard choice. He had run away as a boy. He had avoided facing Mean Jack and rather than face real or imagined consequences of Mean Jack's death, he had runaway again. Jim went to the mess hall to tell Gabe. "Gabe, I'm taking out. Haven't got time to explain but I've got to git before Volkmar finds out. Come with me, will you?" Jim nearly begged. "Where you going?" Gabe asked.

"Don't know. Probably south." Said Jim knowing how Gabe hated the cold .

"Where south?" Gabe trying to decide really didn't care much. Should he follow his friend or stay in the relative security of the camp? He knew things weren't too good for blacks in the South. While Jim had used that destination to appeal to Gabe, it wasn't near as attractive as he might think.

"Look, Gabe . I haven't got time for you to take all day in deciding. Are you coming or not?" Jim was growing impatient to move out.

"Okay, let's go." Gabe turned and lowered the fires on the evening meal he was preparing. He wanted to make sure that the men didn't have a burned meal on his account.

Then the two hurried out the door to the bunkhouse to gather their slim belongings. A few hours later, in the dark they headed on a freight south toward Minneapolis.

"Gabe," said Jim contemplatively, "Why is it we seem to be constantly on a freight headed to who knows where?"

"Cause we're hoboes," said Gabe, "and that's what we is and what we'll probably always be.

"Maybe," said Jim. "Maybe." But a seed had been planted. If nurtured properly, it might grow. Actually, it took the nurturing of a rare mineral - a Ruby.

In Minneapolis, the sun dawned bright and cold - near zero. Across the freight yard smoke was rising from chimneys serving the barracks of an army camp, Camp Snelling.

"Let's git out of this damn cold boxcar and see if we can't scrounge some hot grub" said Gabe, his teeth chattering.

"Anything to move and get warm" Jim answered. "Think they might let loose of a hot meal if we do a little work for 'em?" "Maybe. Sure won't hurt tryin."

The two wandered up to the camp gate. "Where do you think you two are going?" the sergeant of the guard demanded.

"Just lookin for work," said Jim.

."The only work here is soldiering and if you're interested in that go down to that big white building and ask for Sergeant Grayson."

Jim looked at Gabe and Gabe looked at Jim. "What the hell" said Gabe, "Sure beats standing around here freezing to death." That afternoon the two were sworn in.

September 12, 1933

"Tomatoes are cheaper! Potatoes are cheaper! Now's the time to fall in love!" Jim and his buddies were singing at the top of their lungs. The speak easy was filled with cigarette smoke, good looking nurses and drunken soldiers. The nurses came from Perry Point Veteran Hospital and the soldiers from Aberdeen Proving Grounds. The speakeasy was halfway in between at Harve de Grace, Maryland at the northern most point of the Chesapeake Bay.

Gabe had become a cook and was stationed at Camp Polk in Louisiana. Jim had joined the cavalry, but his experience with Bunyon and others of his ilk soon caused him to change to ordnance. After all he was a good mechanic. Jim loved the ordnance and for the first time in his life began to feel successful. He took naturally to small arms. His math skills were honed even to the point of differential calculus, and soon he mastered the art of trajectory prediction. He was teaching at the Ordnance School in Aberdeen and was a good instructor at that.

Gabe was equally successful at Camp Polk. Soon he was running his own mess as mess sergeant. With this promotion came promotion to sergeant first class and all thoughts of returning to the hobo life ended. He now thought of himself as a non-commissioned officer, Besides, the sanctuary of Camp Polk protected him from the racism beginning to grow throughout the country, but especially in the south. Jim and Gabe still kept close by letter and telephone. And Jim felt good about Gabe's promotion and toasted him over the phone with a glass of prohibition rum. Now Jim's promotion to sergeant first class was the excuse for the raucous behavior of he and his buddies this evening.

Ruby sat in a corner with two of her nurse friends. She was small, barely five feet tall, and slim. Her face was round and her eyes and mouth perpetually smiling. Her hair was dark brown but prematurely streaked white in a most attractive fashion. She had been asked a thousand times if she didn't bleach the streak, which she didn't. Ruby had grown up in a small farm town, Cottage Grove in western Tennessee. She was the second youngest of eight children and the love shared by all of them was deep and abiding. Only recently had her applecart been tipped. Her father's flour mill failed three years prior as wheat and corn crops had been replaced by cotton. The children, most of them near grown, were forced to go to work in the cotton mill in Paris, Tennessee, to support the family. Then her mother died. Her uncle, a doctor, seeing the deep depression suffered by Ruby's father, decided to take things into his own hands. He took Ruby and her younger sister Pauline to Memphis and enrolled them in the Baptist Hospital Nursing School. Ruby was a natural. She was a hard worker and, more importantly, a very caring person. When they graduated, Pauline went to work for her uncle and Ruby, in the boldest decision of her young life, took a job at the Perry Point Veterans Hospital, a thousand miles from home. She had spotted Jim and more than once their eyes had met. She thought to herself, "That's really not a bad looking guy, but his voice is atrocious." Embarrassed by her thoughts, she sought to hide behind her glass.

She looked up and suddenly Jim was beside her. "What's your name?" She was stunned and said nothing immediately. Jim flushed and said "I'm sorry. I've . . uh . . ah hell! I didn't mean to . . ." Jim started to turn back to his friends.

"Ruby!" She almost shouted it to stop him from turning away. "My name is Ruby. What's yours?"

"Jim." he answered and smiled. "Would you like to dance, Ruby?" A small band was playing above the din and a few couples were moving about in rough approximation to the rhythm.

"Ok, Jim, I'd love to but I'm not much of a dancer." Ruby rose and they made their way to the dance floor.

Mutt and Jeff, some called them. Jim was over six feet tall and Ruby a foot shorter. A few months later, Jim struggled with a decision. Should he take on the responsibilities of a wife or run away as before. Their romance had flourished at an astonishing rate. They laughed together, played together, explored together and eventually became one together. He reached his decision. Gabe got a call and, his furlough granted, boarded a train headed northeast. He would witness the marriage of his best friend and the jewel - Ruby.

July 14, 1943

Humid. Hot and humid. The afternoon rain hadn't begun and that period just preceding was almost unbearable. It was New Guinea and things were not going well. Supplies were short, and the struggle to get them to the front was near impossible. Delays, mixed priorities, bad planning, and worse roads complicated Jim's job as ordnance officer of the 7th Infantry Division. Jim had been promoted to 1st lieutenant by presidential appointment at the outset of the war and his knack at problem solving propelled him quickly to major. The Army had to transition from a small peacetime closely knit family, to the world's most powerful fighting force, and do it quickly. The task fell to the newly commissioned officers of the old army to train the nearly five million young men to be soldiers of the new Army. On top of that, America's factories were pouring out new war machines to modernize what had been a largely horse-drawn affair. In a year the task was nearly completed, but at the price of great personal sacrifices.

Ruby and Jim had met with some problems. Jim blamed it on their whirlwind romance. Maybe they hadn't gotten to know one another well enough after all. Even ten years into the marriage he was struggling with commitment. Like Bunyon, Jim had balked as Ruby was trying to lead him further down the road of their love where Jim could unload his burdens and share his fears. Jim wouldn't yield beyond a certain point. Frustrated and angry, Ruby fought.

In January 1943, non-compromising Jim asked for the assignment that would take him to the South Pacific. It wasn't easy but through finagling, horse trading and just plain conning, Jim arranged that Gabe should be the mess sergeant at Headquarters Company, 7th Infantry Division. Once again the two friends were roving together - this time they traded the vastness of America's prairies to the vastness of the great Pacific Ocean. Every evening when he was not visiting the front or back at corps, Jim would visit Gabe and the two would talk. Jim talked of Ruby's stubbornness and the fact that she wanted to rein him in. Gabe didn't comment on Ruby. He felt it really wasn't his business. But he did note that since Jim had met her, he had sure matured and that maturation was at her loving hands.

Ruby furnished the love and constancy missing in Jim's life. At each fork Jim had turned towards flight and away from commitment. Impulsively, he consistently had taken the easier of the two paths. Impulse had even had a part in his decision to marry. Even as Jim had dealt with Bunyon with kicks and curses, Ruby dealt with Jim with patience and love. Ruby and Jim wrote. Jim weekly and Ruby daily. Ruby, always careful not to raise any issues of commitment, kept her letters loving and upbeat. Jim's letters were more of what was going on and as a result were well censored. Sometimes an entire page would be blacked out. But at the end of his letters he added words of love and Ruby thought she could detect some movement on his part toward taking the next step. But perhaps that was just wishful thinking on her part.

Jim drove his jeep toward Biak where X Corps

Headquarters was located. He was carrying a footlocker full of unfilled parts orders for the division and was determined to have it out with the Corps Ordnance officer. The division was bogged down and Jim was convinced that priorities had to shift toward supplying the parts or otherwise they would have to be pulled out of line. The 7th Infantry Division anchored the X Corps southern flank. Mangrove swamps and almost impenetrable jungle faced the entire division front. The Japanese held on stubbornly as though this hell hole were the gates to Hirohito's Palace. The fighting was the bloodiest the 7th had experienced. To make matters worse, dinge fever and malaria were taking near the toll of small arms fire and artillery.

The breeze generated by the jeep's movement provided some cooling. As he approached the X Corps perimeter, lost in thought Soldiers were scattering. He didn't hear the approaching zero as it dove from behind. The bomb exploded just four yards from Jim's jeep propelling him, jeep and footlocker in three separate parts ten feet up, ten yards forward and ten feet down. Nor did he feel the strong hands that pulled him into a bunker as the zero sought to finish his work, strafing the headquarters and the airstrip.

All was white. He blinked, trying to clear the view but everything stayed white. "Jim, you ok?" a familiar voice close by said.

"Gabe? that you?" Jim answered.

"Boy, thought you'd done bought the farm and all the chickens and horses with it." Gabe said. "Now take it easy and be still. You're pretty banged up, but I 'spect you'll be alright. Still got some bandages round your head and eyes. "Jim thought, 'well at least that accounted for the all white view.' "You been in a hospital here at corps for three days and they're shipping you back stateside tomorrow. Jim, I got a few things to say real quick so don't interrupt. "These past few years we been growing; you're no longer a hobo who can't stand responsibility. You're a soldier - an officer, and a damn good one at that. And a bit lucky too. Because you found yourself a jewel - a Ruby. Jim, she's just right for you. Now listen, you and me, we're going to be like brothers forever, but you and Ruby . . .well there's something there for you, Jim, that you got to commit to, to find. I know it!" Gabe had finished.

On his long way back home, Jim thought about his friend's words, "Commit to find." Commitment. Should it be so hard to commit to a life of love with a beautiful, caring woman? Had he run long enough? Wasn't it time to let his reigns be drawn? He reflected on his life and his quest for a free soul. He now realized that his soul could only find freedom total loving trust. Gabe was right., Ruby would now have his all inclusive and never again would be afraid of commitment.

His wounds healed quickly with Ruby's tender loving care.

August 4, 1965

Jim was retired. Their three children were in college and doing well. Ruby and he were preparing to go on vacation. Jim, as usual, was taking control of everything. " Now Ruby, we'll be gone for five days so be sure and call the paper"

Ruby interrupted, "Jim this is not World War III! Were just going on a trip to visit your relatives in Wisconsin . Now relax and enjoy. Don't get so ...so organized." She bent over and kissed him on the lips. Jim smiled. This time he wasn't running away.. He was going home to renew those family ties he'd long since severed. And as Gabe would say, things were going to be just fine.

Glossary

A Rations	Fresh, refrigerated, or frozen foods
A1E	Close Air Support Tactical Air Force Fighter Aircraft
AA	Anti aircraft
A/C	Aircraft Commander
AFB	Air Force Base
AFN	Armed Forces Network (FM Radio Station)
AGL	Above Ground Level
AH1G	Cobra gunship
AK47	Russian or Chinese made 7.62 caliber rifle
ARA	Arial Rocket Artillery
ARVN	Army of the Republic of Vietnam
AH1G	Attack Helicopter armed with mini guns, rockets and a grenade launcher
AO	Area of operations
ASAP	As Soon as Possible
BDA	Battle Damage Assessment
B Rations	Canned or preserved foods
Battery	A unit equivalent in size to a company
C Rations	Individual canned and pre-cooked meals
C-7	Caribou (Aircraft)
C-124	Large Cargo Aircraft (old shaky)
C-130	Hercules (Aircraft)
C-141	Large Cargo Aircraft
CH54	Largest of the cargo helicopters. Aka The Sky Crane.
Charlie	a slang term for the Viet Cong
CH47	Large cargo helicopter. The Chinook.
Chopper	helicopter

CO	Commanding Officer
COL	Colonel
CONUS	The continental United States
CPT	Army Captain
C Rations	Packaged food intended for use in combat.
CSM	Command Sergeant Major
Dust-off	Medical evacuation by helicopter
EOD	Explosive Ordinance Demolition
ETS	Estimated time of separation from military service
F-1	Primary Fire Direction Frequency - Fire Direction Net
F-2	Secondary Fire Direction Frequency - Fire Direction Net
FDO	Artillery Fire Direction Officer
Flack Jacket	A heavy fiber-filled jacket worn to protect against shrapnel.
Flechette	A metal dart similar to a nail with fins first used on artillery used with artillery
G1	General Staff - Personnel Officer
G2	General Staff - Intelligence Officer
G3	General Staff - Operations Officer
G4	General Staff - Logistics Officer
GCA	Ground Controlled Approach Radar that enables aircraft to land in poor weather conditions.
Grunt	An endearing term for an infantry soldier
HE	High Explosive
HIFC	Helicopter Instrument Flight Course
Hot LZ	A landing zone under enemy fire.
HQ	Headquarters
JP4	Jet Propellant, It was a 50-50 kerosene-gasoline blend.
L-19	A small fixed winged aircraft
L-23	A twin engine passenger aircraft
Laager	A temporary encampment

Legion of Merit	Medal awarded for exceptional military service.
LTC	Lieutenant Colonel
LZ	Landing Zone - A small clearing that will accommodate landing helicopters
M16	Automatic 5.56 caliber rifle
M60	Automatic 7.62 caliber machine gun
MACV	Military Assistance Command - Vietnam
MAJ	Major
Mortar	A small weapon that fires high trajectory fire at the enemy.
NVA	North Vietnam Army
PA	Public Announcement system
Poncho Liner	blanket sized liner for the Poncho.
POW	Prisoner of War
PX	Post Exchange. A store selling sundries and other personal items. to soldiers.
R&R	Rest and Relaxation
RPG	Rocket Propelled Grenade
RVN	Republic of Vietnam
SGT	Sergeant
Steel Pot	Standard issue steel helmet
SOP	Standing Operating Procedures
S1	Personnel Officer
S2	Intelligence Officer
S3	Operations Officer
S4	Logistics Officer
Short Timer	Soldier approaching his rotation date.
TOC	Tactical Operations Center
UHF	Ultra High Frequency
UH1B	Huey helicopter (equipped with the Lycoming T53-L-5 engine)
UH1C	Huey helicopter (slightly more horsepower than B model)
UH1D	Huey helicopter (much larger cargo compartment)

USMA	United States Military Academy
VC	Viet Cong
XM-3	Model number for rocket pods mounted on the Huey helicopter
XO	Executive Officer. Second in command of a unit.